A Future for North Harris:

The North Harris Trust

Janet Hunter

Published by:
North Harris Trust
Old Hostel
Tarbert
Isle of Harris
HS3 3BG.

ISBN: 978-0-955776-60-1

British Library Cataloguing in Publication Data. A CIP record
for this book can be obtained from the British Library.

Designed and typeset in Sabon by Two Ravens Press.
Cover photograph by Rod Huckbody; cover design
by Two Ravens Press: www.tworavenspress.com

Printed on Forest Stewardship Council-accredited paper by
Biddles Ltd., King's Lynn, Norfolk.

Mixed Sources

Product group from well-managed
forests, controlled sources and
recycled wood or fiber
www.fsc.org Cert no. TT-COC-002303
© 1996 Forest Stewardship Council
FSC

About the Author

Janet Hunter was born and brought up in Stornoway. After completing an M.A. degree at Aberdeen University, she taught briefly in Aberdeen, Stornoway and Inverness. She and her husband then moved back to Aberdeen where they now live. Once her family had grown up, she returned to the University of Aberdeen where she took an M.A. (Hons) in Gaelic Studies. The subject of her M. Litt. thesis was 'Local History Societies (Comuinn Eachdraidh) in the Western Isles.' She taught for some years in the Department of Celtic in the University and has retained a close connection with the Islands. Over the last forty years she and her husband have returned at least twice a year to spend some weeks in Harris. Janet Hunter is the author of *The Islanders and the Orb – The History of the Harris Tweed Industry, 1835-1995.*

Contents

Acknowledgments

I am most grateful to all those who helped me in researching the history of the buy-out of the North Harris Estate and in preparing this book. In particular, I am indebted to Duncan MacPherson, who recorded meticulously the Minutes of Trust and Steering Group meetings and answered my questions about them. John Watt and Sandra Holmes were patience personified as I struggled to understand the technicalities involved in a buy-out. Simon Fraser put himself to considerable trouble to help me and to answer my questions about legal aspects of the buyout. Mary MacLennan, Alistair MacLeod and David Cameron of the North Harris Trust were patient and very supportive throughout the long process of gathering information. All those I interviewed gave me a warm and friendly welcome and helpful information. I was enthused time and again by the undoubted sincerity of all who had committed themselves to achieving a new beginning for North Harris. My heartfelt thanks go to:

David Cameron, Sandy Cumming, Simon Fraser, Nigel Hawkins, Sandra Holmes, James Hunter, Bill Lawson, Calum MacDonald, Donnie MacDonald, John Archie MacDonald, Barbara MacKay, Calum Mackay, Donald Mackay, Iain MacKay, Kenny MacKay, Annchris Maclean, Calum Maclennan, Carol Anne MacLennan, David MacLennan, Mary MacLennan, Norman MacLennan, D. J. MacLeod, Alistair MacLeod, Duncan MacPherson, Alasdair Morrison, Cathie Bell Morrison, John Murdo Morrison, Murdo Morrison, Morag Munro, Ian Robertson, Ian Scarr-Hall, Tony Scherr, David Taylor, John Watt and Brian Wilson.

I hope that I have not omitted anyone whose name should be in the above list. I also hope that I have given an accurate account of events. If I have omitted anyone or been inaccurate, I apologise!

Abbreviations

CLU	Community Land Unit
CnES	Comhairle nan Eilean Siar
HDL	Harris Development Ltd
HIE	Highlands and Islands Enterprise
ISH	Ian Scarr-Hall
JMT	John Muir Trust
NHCSG	North Harris Community Steering Group
NHT	North Harris Trust
NOP	New Opportunities Fund
SLF	Scottish Land Fund
SNH	Scottish Natural Heritage
SOS	*Scotland on Sunday*
SSSI	Sites of Special Scientific Interest
WHFP	*West Highland Free Press*
WIE	Western Isles Enterprise
WIIC	Western Isles Islands Council

List of Photographs

Introduction

*'If we miss this chance, we may never have it
again. We have been happy with Bulmer, but what
if someone else comes in – what then? It's a big
undertaking, and we have to take it step by step.'*

So said Kenny Mackay, Chairman of Harris Development Ltd.,
when the people of North Harris were at the early stages of
discussing a community buy-out of the estate. Perhaps surprisingly
to those who are cynical about the whole concept of people
owning the land on which they live and work, the motivation
in North Harris was never 'revenge.' As one woman said,

> *'Yes, the Clearances should not be forgotten, but
> they are part of history. The Land Wars were not
> in the minds of people who formed the Trust. You
> cannot live on revenge.'*

On the contrary, the words used most frequently in the context of
the buy-out echo the sentiments expressed by Kenny Mackay:

> *'The future, opportunity, responsibility, obligation,
> duty, using our resources for the benefit of the
> people.'*

It is stating the obvious to say that North Harris was not another
Assynt, nor yet another Eigg. There was little of the high emotion
of those community buy-outs in which anti-landlord feeling was
paramount. The recent landowner of the North Harris Estate had
not incurred the distrust and dislike, the contempt and resentment
evoked by exploitative landlords in earlier buy-outs such as Eigg
or Assynt. From the outset of negotiations, Jonathan Bulmer, the
landowner of North Harris, reciprocated the goodwill of the
community with a sympathetic attitude to their aspirations. The
moving spirit which inspired the advocates of the North Harris
buy-out seems to have been a determination to take responsibility

for their own future and that of the generations to come. While the reactions of local people in North Harris to the proposed buy-out ranged from the enthusiastic through the cautiously positive to the instinctively negative, an open-minded willingness to listen to the case and a hard-headed realism as to the implications of buying the estate were the predominant attitudes.

News that the North Harris Estate was about to come on the market became known in the Western Isles on Thursday, 25th April 2002. By February 2003, the people of North Harris knew that their efforts over the previous ten months to buy the estate had been successful. They had bought the land on which they lived. The story of how that was achieved has been recorded here for a variety of reasons: it is recorded, in part because even the most vivid memories fade over time; in part in the hope that it may provide inspiration to other communities aspiring to follow the example of North Harris, and in part in the hope that it will go some way to counteracting some of the clichés churned out by the tabloids about the island and its people.

As seems to be inevitable where the Highlands are concerned, press coverage of the negotiations ranged from the responsible and sympathetic to the lurid and sensational. All the ingredients were readily available to those who wanted to sensationalise the story: a fairy-tale Victorian castle, a landowner whose personal circumstances could be exploited to satisfy those readers who revel in the misfortunes of others, rugged Highland peasants to be portrayed as latter-day heroes of the 19th century Crofters' War re-visited – or, worse still, as Mugabe-style land-grabbers. There was a roll-call of celebrities from Nick Faldo to Madonna, each of whom was allegedly interested in buying the land as a hideaway, and above all there was the barren beauty of the land itself.

Much of the serious press coverage did, quite justifiably, emphasise the landscape, the beauty of the scenery, the unspoiled environment, the wilderness (a relatively new concept) and, inevitably, the alarming decline in population. In contrast to those intangible aspects of North Harris, there was little analysis in the press of the mundanities of day-to-day survival by people who had committed themselves to earning a livelihood on an island in which there was a fragile economy, a scarcity of affordable housing, a lack of recreational amenities, a high cost for transport (which affects the cost of living in every sphere) and a harsh climate – all of which encouraged many young people to opt for life in the island capital Stornoway, or further afield on the mainland.

One of the most startling facts to emerge in the research for this book was that a significant number of people employed in Tarbert, and elsewhere in Harris, have to commute from Stornoway – some forty to fifty miles over the heights of the Clisham. This is because their homes are not in Harris where they work, but somewhere in Lewis, and this journey can require up to an hour's driving, much of it on single track roads, and often in weather which would otherwise have '*Dangerous driving conditions*' flashing on our television screens or motorway roadside warnings. Quite apart from the inconvenience of this commuting is the fact that it deprives North Harris of an input from those commuters into the social life of the community and, more importantly, of the presence of their children growing up in Harris.

Concern that the next owner of North Harris might not be as benevolent as Jonathan Bulmer was certainly valid in light of previous history: for example, the German artist, Maruma, who bought Eigg; or, closer to home, Nazmudin Virani, who bought the Island of Scarp with a view to building a luxury hotel and casino there. It was also valid in the context of housing and employment: the need to retain a young population and the need to develop the assets of North Harris were the most important considerations for those committed to buying the land. Without any bitterness, one commentator said of the succession of landowners in North Harris that 'the worst they did was nothing and the best they did was nothing.'

It stands to reason that any private landowner, however wealthy he may be, has his own economic well-being as his primary concern. While landowners might quibble at charges that they were doing nothing when in fact they thought they were doing their best, and critics of landowners might feel that they were let off lightly at that, it is undeniable that a new energy and self-motivation to develop the natural resources of North Harris have been unleashed since the community has taken over responsibility for the land.

Until 1970, it was accepted almost as a law of nature that Harris and the Southern Isles should be part of Inverness-shire and should be governed in every material respect from Inverness, while Lewis should be part of Ross-shire and be governed from Dingwall. These islands suffered generations of neglect and were expected to be grateful for the scrapings from the bottom of the barrel for provision of all the amenities which mainland communities took for granted. Worst of all was the fact that young people were weaned away from the islands for education and jobs. With the creation of Comhairle nan Eilean Siar as an All-Purpose Authority in 1975, to take responsibility for governing the islands in all matters out with national government, a new surge of energy, self-confidence and self-respect was to be felt throughout the Western Isles. Schools, roads – even a road to Rhenigidale – and many other improvements in the standard of living have come to be taken for granted, as they should be in any civilised modern community.

A similar injection of energy, along with a sense of purpose and self-confidence, is already manifesting itself because of the decision to place responsibility for the future of North Harris into the hands of the people themselves. This book tells the story of how the community of North Harris reached for and achieved that success.

The History of the Estate

Harris was, until the eighteenth century, part of the clan territory of the MacLeods of Dunvegan. As early as the mid-seventeenth century, particularly harsh attitudes to the tenantry were becoming apparent in both Harris and Dunvegan. According to the Gaelic poet the Blind Harper in his *Oran do Mhac Leòid Dhùn Bheagain,* the young chief Roderick MacLeod squandered the income from his estates on conspicuous extravagance and high living in the south, and raised the rents to meet his expenditure. Eventually, the debts on the estate were such that Harris was sold in 1779 to Captain Alexander, a son of the MacLeod tacksman in Berneray. Although Captain Alexander spent money on developing the fishing in Harris, his son Norman Hume MacLeod doubled the rents and forced the tenants into kelping for its enormous – but short-term – profitability. Under Alexander Norman MacLeod, who succeeded his father Alexander Hume MacLeod, the whole of North Harris from Hushinish to Kinlochresort was cleared in 1811. The people were removed from Cliasmol, as it was to be let as a sheep farm. Horgabost, Luskentyre, Scarista Bheag, Scarista Mhòr and Rodel were treated just as harshly. The nineteenth century was one of inexorable economic decline for the ordinary people of Harris.

Sheep became the principal source of income, and to make available extensive sheep walks and thereby charge the highest possible rents, the people were moved to the least fertile margins of the estate. The harsh treatment meted out to the tenantry and the suffering endured by the people who had been cleared were graphically recalled by old men giving evidence to the Napier Commission in 1884. Summarily expelled from their homes and cultivated land, they were forced to scrape a living from the boulder-strewn lunar landscape of the coastal fringes on the east of Harris, where the remains of lazy-beds still testify to the effort needed to raise a meagre crop from the thin acid soil. Alternatively, they were crowded into the islands of Scalpay and Scarp. Despite the wholesale clearance of Harris for sheep in the early nineteenth century, Alexander Norman MacLeod was bankrupt by 1830. In 1834, the estate was sold to the fifth Earl of Dunmore. In that year, the debts secured on the Harris estate were almost £27,000 in excess of the price of £60,210 which the sale realised.

It goes without saying that all the MacLeod owners of Harris had been absentee landowners, and that situation did not change with the advent of the Dunmore family. Sheep were still seen as a profitable commodity, and clearance continued until the mid-nineteenth century. Many of the displaced tenants were cleared to the Bays of Harris or were forced to emigrate to Cape Breton or, worse still in their eyes, to Australia. The running of the estate was left to the Factors or Baillies whose duty it was to make the land as profitable as possible. Harris had its share of sadistic factors who seemed to delight in persecuting the tenantry. Stories still linger in the oral tradition about the self-serving Donald Stewart, one of the more infamous factors to the Earl of Dunmore. At a time when the rights of the property-owning class and their representatives were paramount, and when poverty was equated with moral depravity, there were few to challenge the petty tyrants who held sway over the small tenants of Highland Scotland.

The people of Harris suffered serious hardship throughout the Potato Famine from 1846 till 1851: seven full years of constant hunger, diseases such as typhus, measles and influenza exacerbated by malnutrition. T. M. Devine in the Appendix to *The Great Highland Famine* quotes from the Scotsman of 12 December 1846, saying that the number of deaths from 'dysentry and British cholera were increasing with fearful rapidity among the cottar class.' (Devine, 1988, p.309-310). The self-aggrandising attitude of many nineteenth-century Highland landowners, the Dunmores among them, can be deduced from apparently innocuous incidents. While Lord Dunmore's kitting out of all his ghillies and keepers in Murray tartan tweed in the 1830s did have the benefit of being the catalyst for the Harris Tweed industry, the wanton extravagance of Charles, 7th Earl of Dunmore, as he strove to impress his young wife, brought about the break-up of the estate and the sale of North Harris to Sir Edward Scott. Just after his coming of age, Charles had a castle built at Ardvourlie. However, as it was inconvenient for his hunting activities, a grander castle was built at Amhuinnsuidhe – originally called Fincastle after his own courtesy title as oldest son of an Earl of Dunmore, but the name was later changed to Amhuinnsuidhe Castle. According to oral tradition his young wife Gertrude, a daughter of the Earl of Leicester, was singularly unimpressed with Amhuinnsuidhe Castle, comparing it unfavourably to a hen-house or stable at her father's home. The story goes that Charles then built another wing onto Amhuinnsuidhe, and that final expenditure on top of all he had already spent on building two castles within a decade, led to his bankruptcy. True, or exaggerated with the passage of time, one simply has to look around these castles to realise that importing the building materials by sea and employing armies of craftsmen must surely have stretched the Dunmore purse.

When sheep farming became less profitable in the mid-nineteenth century, deer forests had been created for the entertainment of the landowner and his guests. According to a later Factor for North Harris, Robert Matheson, who gave evidence to the Deer Forest Commissioners in 1892, the Forest of Harris had been formed in the 1850s from land which had been cleared for sheep farms some thirty years previously. (Lawson, *Harris in History and Legend*, p. 146.) The hope of restoration of that land which had been tenanted by their grandfathers was the reason for the landless cottars continuing their struggle, despite the Crofters' Act of 1886. The frivolous use of land which could have been made available to cottars was bitterly condemned by the Land League in the 1880s and much resented by cottars on all estates, as exemplified by the Pàirc Deer raid across the border in Lewis.

While stories of Dunmore profligacy passed down in the oral tradition may owe something to the re-telling, the survey of the Dunmore estate conducted by the Land Court appointed by the Crofters' Commission showed in 1891 that the rents levied in South Harris had been excessive. As a result of the investigations made by the Commission, 87% of rent arrears were cancelled and the remaining rents were reduced by on average 48½%.

Those reductions were the greatest in the Hebrides. (Macphail, *The Crofters' War*, 1989, p. 175.)

Whatever the facts behind the stories, Charles, 7th Earl of Dunmore, sold North Harris – including Scalpay, Scarp and the village of Tarbert – in 1868 to Sir Edward Scott, a London banker.

The voice which is recorded for posterity in Highland Scotland is not, as a rule, that of the Gaelic-speaking lower orders, but that of the English-speaking establishment, the deferential press, ministers of the church, estate factors and external observers. It has become an accepted fact – which one questions at one's peril – that both Sir Edward Scott and his son Sir Samuel were, as landowners go, benevolent owners. The undoubted poverty and harsh living conditions of the small tenants in North Harris described in evidence to both the Napier Commission of 1884 and the Deer Forest Commission ten years later, compel closer examination of that accepted 'fact.'

The Scotts' reputation may have been fortuitously enhanced by the changing political sympathies in the last decade of the nineteenth and the first two decades of the twentieth centuries. The crofting community was to some extent on the conscience of both the liberal press and a national government under pressure from militant cottars waging an increasingly desperate land struggle. The efforts of Government to appease the land lobby are shown by the number of commissions of enquiry and the range of crofting legislation passed between 1886 and 1919. It seems as if the Scotts were relatively responsive to the more liberal attitudes in their dealings with the tenants on their North Harris estate.

In the 1870s, just after Sir Edward Scott had become owner of North Harris, the land struggle began to gain momentum in the Highlands – particularly in Skye. In Lewis, just across the boundary, in the trial of the so-called Bernera Rioters in 1873, Donald Munro, Factor to Sir James Matheson, was shown to have persecuted the Lewis tenantry. Within ten years of that trial, land agitation had reached the point at which the Government was forced to set up a Royal Commission of Enquiry into the condition of the Crofters and Cottars in the Highlands (The

Napier Commission). After two years of escalating tension and protest at the lack of action, the crucial Crofters' Act was passed in 1886.

Questioned by The Napier Commission in 1883, witnesses in North Harris testified that their impoverished circumstances had not been inflicted on them by the then landowner, Sir Edward Scott, but by earlier factors to the Earls of Dunmore. Sir Edward Scott died in 1883, and thereafter the estate was managed by his trustees, including Lady Scott and her brother Mr Edward Packe, during the minority of Sir Samuel Scott. (Duncan, *A Hebridean Island: Memories of Scarp*, p. 74.) From the evidence given to the Napier Commission in Tarbert in June 1883, it is clear that serious 'overcrowding on the land, the scantiness of the land, and its inadequacy to maintain the people' had contributed to their 'poor circumstances.' To take but one example, evidence given to the Napier Commission sixteen years into the Scotts' ownership of North Harris showed that the people of Ardhasaig were 'very much hemmed and crowded in.'

> 'We who are without land are a burden upon those who have a little of it; and if it were not that they accommodate us out of their little by giving us potato ground we would have starved in a heap.' (Report of the Napier Commission, qq. 17715-17782.)

A similar story was repeated from other villages such as Scalpay and Scarp.

Living conditions for crofters in Harris, as in the rest of the Highlands and Islands, were slightly easier after the Crofters' Act of 1886. While security of tenure was undoubtedly an important clause in the Crofters' Act, the most immediate relief was achieved by the decision of the Land Court, established under the Act to reduce exorbitant rents and, where they saw fit, to cancel altogether some rent arrears. The great omission of the Act was the failure to return land taken in the clearances. The result of this omission was to condemn the landless cottars of Harris and elsewhere to another two generations of marginal subsistence and dependence on the generosity of the neighbouring crofters.

The example of the land raiders in Pàirc, and later those at Aignish in Lewis, was not altogether lost on the cottars of Harris, where there was acute poverty and suffering among the landless population. However, it may be that the prison sentences imposed on the Lewis activists were sufficient to deter actual seizure of land in Harris. Desperate though they must have been, the Harris cottars merely petitioned the Factor to ask for more land for small tenants, and they even went as far as to threaten one particularly unpopular sheep farmer. The Medical Officer for North Harris thought that it was not surprising that there should be threats 'to imitate the Lewis men' from the cottar population. (Hunter, J. *The Making of the Crofting Community*, 1976, p. 176.)

The reputation for benevolence of the Scott family may lie as much in their willingness, in the mid-1880s, to create a limited number of new holdings in North Harris, as in the provision of a school inTarbert and, in 1900, the provision of a carding mill in Tarbert by Sir Samuel Scott.

In his book *Harris in History and Legend*, Bill Lawson of *Cò Leis Thu?* gives details of the resettlement of the Forest of Harris in the 1880s. In 1884, Bowglas and Scaladale were taken out of the Deer Forest and resettled, and in 1885 Maaruig was resettled for six tenants, five of whom were from Scalpay. (Lawson, p.165.) Lady Scott supplied four of the tenants from Scalpay with a cow, or with money to buy one. (Lawson, p. 166.) She also made potato ground at Hushinish available rent-free to the people of Scarp. (Lawson, p.152.) Another four from Scalpay were resettled on new crofts at Ardvourlie. (Lawson, p. 165.) It may be that this resettlement was not quite as amicable as the written sources imply; the family traditions of Murdo Morrison of Ardvourlie (who was to become one of the Directors of the North Harris Trust) maintain that an ancestor was one of two men from Bowglass who raided Ardvourlie and staked out crofts, thereby incurring serious opposition from the Estate. The family stories of physical fighting over the claims to crofts suggest that the land hunger in North Harris was not allayed by the creation of a small number of holdings. Bedersaig was resettled in 1885, as were Direascal and Luachair on Loch Resort – although these people were moved again to crofts at Hushinish when the farm there was broken up in 1900. (Lawson, p. 156.) Interestingly, the re-settlement of Cliasmol did not take place until 1919, after the Great War, when land hunger was again making itself actively felt. (Lawson, p. 148.)

It is worth noting that witnesses from Scalpay and Scarp had testified before the Napier Commission to the desperate overcrowding of those two islands. Despite the Scotts' attempts to meet the most pressing needs of cottars in Scalpay, several families from Scalpay emigrated to the Falklands and Patagonia in the late 1880s and 1890s. In 1900, there was a relocation of families from Rhenigidale to Fiscavaig in Skye, and another from Scalpay to North Uist in the 1920s. Both were sponsored by the Board of Agriculture, which at the time was valiantly trying to fulfil the recruitment promise of land for all ex-servicemen. (Lawson, 1990, *Harris Families and How to Trace Them.*)

A tribute to Sir Samuel's generosity toward his Harris tenants was paid in 1919, in connection with Ardhasaig Farm. In 1913, Ardhasaig was considered for new smallholdings, but as the land was poor and it was a sporting property, the cost of providing deer fences and compensation to the estate seemed prohibitive to the Board of Agriculture. Ardhasaig Farm was raided in 1915, but the raiders were offered work building a new road, and the trouble died down for a while. In 1919, Ardhasaig Farm was raided again, but unlike many contemporary owners, Sir Samuel declined to take legal action and asked Thomas Wilson (the area representative for the Board of Agriculture) to investigate the creation of new holdings. Wilson reported that it was a difficult problem, as almost every square inch of land in North Harris which could be utilised for smallholdings was already in the hands of crofters. Nonetheless, he worked out a scheme for fifteen new holdings, and advised the Board to approve them as soon as possible. Wilson added,

'I should mention that the action of Sir Samuel Scott
in agreeing to the above proposals is most generous,
and he should receive the Board's recognition of
this. Undoubtedly, had compulsory powers been

resorted to he would have received very large awards for damage to the Forest Shootings and Fishings ... probably so high that it could have proved impossible to proceed with any scheme of smallholdings.' (Leneman, *Fit for Heroes?* pp. 125-126.)

Sir Samuel Scott would seem to have felt genuine affection for his tenantry, and regret at having to sell the North Harris Estate in 1919. A measure of that affection for Harris could be sensed in his retention of Amhuinnsuidhe Castle on a fifteen-year lease. In words which presaged the dilemma of North Harris in 2002, Sir Samuel explained in a letter to his tenants in both English and Gaelic, his reasons for selling to Lord Leverhulme:

' *..After long talks with Lord Leverhulme, I was convinced that in him you would have a Proprietor who would further your interests and do all in his power, far more than I could ever do, to help you. At my death the estate would have had to be sold, and I believed it best for you all that the estate should be sold to a man who will be a good and generous landlord, than that it should be sold after my death to some unknown person who might not have had your interests at heart.'* (Nicolson, *Lord of the Isles*, p.122.)

Nonetheless, in 1919 Sir Samuel Scott was in his mid-forties, some twenty years younger than Lord Leverhulme. One must wonder why he anticipated that he should be the one to die first. As it happened, he outlived Lord Leverhulme by almost twenty years.

By any criteria, Sir Samuel Scott would seem to have had good reason for his belief that Lord Leverhulme would be a generous landlord, with the interests of his tenantry at heart. Leverhulme's treatment of his workers at Port Sunlight was seen as a model of benevolence, and his plans for Lewis and Harris promised an injection of sorely-needed development capital. In

1919, no-one was to know that the greater part of Leverhulme's philanthropy in Harris was to be in Leverburgh rather than in Tarbert. His intention was to raise the people's standard of living by giving them employment in public works, modernising the Harris tweed industry through supplying mill-spun yarn rather than the traditional hand-spun yarn and, in particular, by transforming the fishing industry from a base at Leverburgh. (Nicolson, *Lord of the Isles*, p. 213.) In none of these aims did he succeed. Although there was a demand for crofts, particularly at Rodel, the community and the Board of Agriculture preferred not to risk alienating Leverhulme, who was vehemently opposed to the crofting system, by creating new crofts as had been done in Lewis. The result was that by 1925, although 337 applications had been received under the Small Landholders' Act of 1911, only 59 new holdings or extensions of crofts had been granted in Harris: a percentage of 17.5 %, compared with 40% in Lewis, Skye and the Uists. (Hutchison, *The Soap Man*, p. 177.)

North Harris did benefit briefly from Leverhulme's expenditure on the Whaling Station at Bunabhainneadar on West Loch Tarbert. Bought from a Norwegian company, the repair work on the decaying factory provided much-needed employment; but from the start of operations the whaling station was a financial failure, as there was no market for the inedible whale meat canned there. The smell of the processing of the carcasses still lingers in the memory of those old enough to remember the factory at work. When a catastrophic slump hit the market for Harris Tweed, the only other major source of employment, Leverhulme felt bound to provide alternative work in the form of much-needed road-making. He offered to share with the Scottish Office the cost of constructing three roads: a six-mile stretch from Tarbert to Kyles Scalpay, a four-mile stretch from near Amhuinnsuidhe to Hushinish opposite the Island of Scarp, and a five-mile stretch from Leverburgh to Finsbay. (Nicolson, *Lord of the Isles*, p. 222.)

As well as providing employment, the construction of these roads eased living conditions for the communities involved. For instance, the two hundred people of Scarp had to fetch all their supplies by boat from Tarbert and, when stormy weather made it too dangerous to launch a boat, they faced near-starvation – as described so graphically by Angus Duncan in his book, *A Hebridean Island: Memories of Scarp*. By Leverhulme's guarantee that he would pay half the cost of three of the four roads being built in Harris in 1924, every workless man in Harris was provided with employment. According to his biographer Nigel Nicolson, despite the fact that he gave money for a recreation hall and a playing field in Tarbert, and contributed to the cost of the War Memorial and a new water supply, the roads that Leverhulme provided in Harris have become his chief legacy to the island. Summing up the difference between Leverhulme in Lewis and Leverhulme in Harris, Nicolson says:

'*In Lewis, it (the crofting system) had filled him more with anger than pity; in Harris he showed more pity than anger.*' (Nicolson, p. 223.)

The model of patriarchal landowners such as Scott or Leverhulme, concerned with the well-being of the tenants, was beginning to give way to that of the landowner as a relatively anonymous seasonal visitor, primarily interested in preserving his privacy and the commercial value of the fishing and shooting on the estate. The roll-call of Harris landowners after Leverhulme becomes quite complicated. Unknown to everyone except his closest advisers, Leverhulme had been in serious financial difficulties in 1920 and 1921, both personally and in Lever Brothers, largely because of unwise investment in the Niger Company. (Nicolson, pp. 165-167.) Within a week of his death in May 1925, all development works were halted and men were given a week's notice, except for those working on construction of the roads for which he had given an undertaking to the Scottish Office. (Nicolson, p. 232.) Although North Harris, Lot 10 of Leverhulme's island properties, was advertised for sale by Messrs. Knight, Frank and Rutley for £61, 850 on Thursday 22nd October 1925, bidding at the auction in London was embarrassingly low.

Amhuinnsuidhe Castle, Ardvourlie Lodge, Harris Hotel and 6000 acres were sold for a mere £2000 (Nicolson, p. 235) to

J. L. Venables who, within the year, sold it back to Sir Samuel Scott, the owner before Leverhulme. (*Third Statistical Account: County of Inverness,* Outer Isles District: The Parish of Harris, p. 567.) J. L. Venables was a property dealer who in 1929 lived in Luskentyre, and later in Kyles Lodge. Sir Samuel continued as owner of North Harris until his death in 1944. His wife, Lady Sophie Scott, predeceased him in 1937. They are both buried in a four-chambered cairn on a hill behind Amhuinnsuidhe Castle, surely a testament to their regard for Harris. Although today the Scotts' largesse in providing salmon and game to the tenants might be scorned, it seems to have been appreciated at the time, as was the ample employment provided for thirty permanent and ten seasonal staff. (Tony Scherr, leaflet on history of Harris, 2003.) This is in marked contrast to later landowners, who would allow the carcasses of deer to rot rather than allow the ordinary people to have them.

After Sir Samuel Scott's death in 1944, North Harris entered a period of relatively short-term ownership by a succession of rather exotic figures. It was first sold to Brockett Estates Ltd. Lord Brockett was better known for his pro-Nazi sympathies before and during the war than for his benevolence to his tenants. Two years later Brockett Estates sold again, this time for £40,000, to Sir Thomas Octave Murdoch (Tommy) Sopwith. (*Third Statistical Account:* Outer Isles District: the Parish of Harris, p. 567.) Sopwith was founder of the Sopwith Aviation and Engineering Company, perhaps best remembered for the eponymous Sopwith Camel. (*Chambers' Biographical Dictionary,* 1969, p. 1196.) A keen yachtsman and competitor for the America Cup, Sopwith employed Harris seamen to crew his yachts. His name lingered on in Harris for many a year in the stories of one particular island member of his crew who, having served on minesweepers protecting the Atlantic convoys during the war, went on to serve on the Sopwith yacht. Among other tales, this seaman-crofter relished telling of the occasion when, berthed in Monte Carlo harbour, he was awakened by a fearful fracas on the pier. In a far cry from both convoys and crofting, he described in detail the expulsion from Monaco by the local gendarmerie of the notorious Lady Docker, whose visit to a casino went sour when she had the temerity to insult the Monegasque flag. Because Sopwith had a high regard for his gamekeeper Fred MacInnes, he allowed him to buy his tied house and some land when the estate was sold, something which the Macinnes family appreciated as well-deserved recognition of their father's skill and dedication to his work. Tommy Sopwith demonstrated his lasting affection for Harris by returning to visit the island when he was 100 years of age. In 1961, Major Potter Miller-Mundy and Captain Lowndes bought North Harris for £80,000, and they were the first proprietors to commercialise the shooting and fishing with paying guests.

The next owners, Sir Hereward and Lady Wake, bought the estate in 1968 and continued the commercialisation by letting the castle along with the shooting and fishings. (Scherr, 2003.) It has been said that the Wakes were the first owners who seemed to actively dislike the tenantry. Such was their antipathy and desire for privacy that Sir Hereward approached Inverness County Council to create a new road round the back of the Castle, to prevent people passing close to the front door. Lord Burton, the then-Chairman of Inverness County Council and coincidentally a fellow old Etonian, sympathised so much with Sir Hereward's dilemma that he was prepared to expend a major part of the Inverness-shire roads budget to oblige his friend. Only a vigorous campaign by the *West Highland Free Press* forced abandonment of that infamous scheme.

One particular incident towards the end of the Hereward Wake era may well have alerted the people of North Harris to the inherent risks of the estate being offered for sale. In September 1975, news broke that an American syndicate was attempting to organise the purchase of the 62,000-acre North Harris Estate. The projected plans for the estate were bizarre, to say the least. The brochure issued by Period Houses of Wisconsin Avenue, Washington said that they intended to turn North Harris into 'a vacation haven and a sporting retreat for the investors themselves,' but that 'a good profit was also offered by running the estate on the basis of a private membership club.' A group of ten Florida investors were said to form the core of the would-be owners of North Harris. The brochure also stated:

'The members of the Florida group are particularly attracted to this estate because it is remote and uncontaminated; rich in unpolluted natural resources that have never been over-used.'

Roy Veatch, the spokesman for Period Houses of Wisconsin Avenue, Washington, said that they meant to keep it that way indefinitely.

'We are thinking in terms of $10,000 shares and we think we have 15 or 20 investors we can count on. We have just finished mailing two important Scottish Societies and we think that would bring in a lot more interest. Most of the interest so far has come from people with Scottish backgrounds. They are all very keen to maintain their links'. The purpose is to develop the sporting aspects of North Harris, and the castle would be used as a lodge.' (West Highland Free Press, 12 September 1975.)

Alarm bells began to ring in Harris, and certainly in Westminster. By September 19 two Scottish MPs, Jim Sillars (South Ayrshire) and Donald Stewart (Western Isles), reacted angrily to the American plans. Jim Sillars called for William Ross, Secretary of State for Scotland, to instruct the Highlands and Islands Board (HIDB) to intervene and acquire the estate. He said, 'The reason it's unpolluted is that nobody's been allowed on it! ... These decisions have to be taken with regard to the interests of the people.' Donald Stewart also called for the Secretary of State or the local authority to intervene: 'It is unthinkable that this estate should fall into the hands of rich Americans or another Hereward Wake.' He thought that the government could be doing more to buy lots of land from out of private landlordism when opportunities presented themselves. *(West Highland Free Press, 19 September, 1975.)* By December, the sorry saga had petered out, with no more than the Island of Scalpay being sold to John Taylor, a partner in a London firm of architects who already owned the nearby island of Scotisay.

The Wake tenure ended in 1976 with the sale of North Harris to a Gerald Panchaud, a businessman from Switzerland who ran the estate much as had the previous two owners. An even more bizarre example of asset-stripping occurred under the Panchauds, when the Island of Scarp was sold for £80,000 to a Mr Nazmudin Virani, who had fled to Britain from Uganda and Idi Amin. It was announced that Mr Virani planned to turn Scarp into a holiday resort, complete with '150 traditional-style Highland cottages to be used as holiday homes to be sold or leased for £1000 a week, a landing strip for private planes, a private jetty, a luxury sports complex with swimming pool, a sauna, a solarium, squash courts and all-weather tennis courts.' (*Press and Journal,* 16 August, 1983.) No doubt Mr Virani was unaware of the wind speed in Scarp. He was also unaware that almost all of Scarp was in crofting tenure and could not be developed as he might have wanted. A post-script to a totally hare-brained scheme, which has echoes of the subsequent Maruma affair in Eigg, came when Mr Virani was sentenced in 1991 to two and a half years imprisonment for fraudulent dealings in the wake of the closure of the Bank of Credit and Commerce International (the notorious BCCI, which had such dire financial repercussions for the Western Isles Islands Council, as it was at that time).

On General Panchaud's death, his widow continued to run the estate for two years. When she sold it to the Bulmer family in 1994, she retained an area of land on the shore of Loch Seaforth along with the mineral rights (Scherr, 2003), a part of the estate which was to be re-united with the rest of North Harris through a second community buy-out in 2006. Jonathan Bulmer was a member of the Bulmer cider family and his wife, Lady Marcia, was a daughter of the late Earl Granville from North Uist. They made their family home in one wing of the Castle, while renting the rest of the castle to sporting parties or paying guests for art courses and the cookery courses made popular through the television programmes 'Castle Cook,' run by Rosemary Schragar. (Scherr, 2003.) As the Bulmers actually lived full-time at the Castle and their children attended the local school, they were more integrated in the community than many of their predecessors.

Chapter 1
The Estate on the Market

Although the media treated it as sensational, the news that Jonathan Bulmer had put Amhuinnsuidhe Estate on the market, inviting offers of £4.5 million, did not come as an absolute bolt from the blue to everyone in Harris on Thursday 25 April 2002. There were some who had been hoping for the sale of the estate for a number of years. What the news of the forthcoming sale did was to have a galvanising effect on those who were aware of the possibilities that the sale offered for the people of the estate.

Any one of half a dozen people might have taken the initiative to organise a meeting to discuss the implications of the sale. As it happened, the person first off the mark was the local Chairman of the Scottish Crofting Foundation, Donald MacLennan, who contacted Alasdair Morrison, MSP for the Western Isles, and the two councillors for Harris on Comhairle nan Eilean Siar (Western Isles Island Council): Morag Munro (Harris West) and Donald Macdonald (Harris East). Following Donald MacLennan's excited phone call, Alasdair Morrison MSP arranged for a meeting to be held in Tarbert Community Centre on the following Monday, 29th April.

The fact that this first meeting was requested by a representative of the crofters in North Harris and convened by the MSP and local Councillors caused a degree of confusion in the community at large as to the purpose of the meeting. It laid undue emphasis on the role of crofting legislation in any potential buy-out and, rather unfortunately, gave the impression that the MSP rather than the community was in the driving seat – something which was resented by a number of people. Despite the aspirations of those who wanted to see some sort of crofter or community buy-out in North Harris, there was no certainty in April 2002 that a buy-out would take place. Most people were, at best, curious as to what the options were, extremely cautious about venturing into unknown territory and, in many cases, reluctant to relinquish the perceived security of the status quo. The most conservative attitudes seemed to emanate from those who lived in close proximity to Amhuinnsuidhe Castle itself, that is the part of North Harris which was immediately identified as 'the Estate,' where Jonathan Bulmer was well-known as a relatively benevolent landowner. The more radical attitudes came from the areas not so readily identified as part of the estate; in fact, the further from the Castle, the more likely people were to consider that a buy-out might have much to recommend it. It was clear that considerable discussion by a wide-cross section of the community was going to be necessary.

Because local newspapers The *Stornoway Gazette* and *The West Highland Free Press* had just been published on the Wednesday and Thursday of that week, those papers missed the opportunity to break the news. However, the rest of the media, particularly the local radio, broadcast the news of the proposed sale and publicised the meeting to be held in Tarbert. Initially, Alasdair Morrison MSP and Donald MacLennan had envisaged simply a meeting between members of the Scottish Crofters' Foundation, local councillors and relevant agencies. Despite the very short notice over the weekend, a public meeting was arranged for the beginning of the following week on Monday 29 April, in Tarbert Community Centre. Between the Thursday and Monday, invitations to attend the meeting were sent to some of the people and agencies best placed to advise the community on the options presented by the sale.

If the local crofters or the community at large were contemplating any kind of action in the purchase of the Estate, it was essential that they should have professional advice from the outset. With this in mind, a range of speakers with relevant expertise was invited to attend the meeting on Monday 29 April. Of these, perhaps the most important adviser was John Watt, Head of the Community Land Unit, a unit established in 1997 by Highlands and Islands Enterprise in order to provide advice and support for community land initiatives such as that offered by the sale of the North Harris Estate.

On the Monday evening, forty people out of a total population of some eight hundred gathered in Tarbert Community Centre

– a number considered quite healthy by local standards. Short notice and the inability of the local weekly papers (which did not come out till the Wednesday and Thursday after the meeting) to publicise the event, seriously affected the turnout. A number of people who would have wanted to be there, did not know that this first meeting was taking place. It may also have been the case that those who were not crofters, and that included almost all the residents of the centre of population in Tarbert itself, considered that the meeting was irrelevant to them if it was simply a meeting of crofters to consider the situation.

Opening that first meeting, Alasdair Morrison MSP in the Chair tried to make amends for the initial confusion over the purpose of the meeting. He explained that, although the original meeting planned with members of the Scottish Crofters' Foundation had been a private meeting, they had quickly realised that an open meeting which included a wider cross-section of the community than just the crofters would be more appropriate. They had also recognised that representatives from Comhairle nan Eilean Siar, Highlands and Islands Enterprise, Western Isles Enterprise and other appropriate agencies should be involved from the beginning. Having introduced the representatives of Comhairle nan Eilean Siar, Western Isles Enterprise, Highlands and Islands Enterprise and other agencies, Alasdair Morrison went on to say that although Jonathon Bulmer had been a good landlord, the sale of Amhuinnsuidhe Estate presented an opportunity to safeguard North Harris from an uncertain future with a new landowner who might be less concerned than Mr Bulmer for the well-being of the estate and its tenants. He assured the audience that the Community Land Unit was available to provide any advice and support that might be needed for a community buy-out.

The first speaker was John Watt, Head of Highlands and Islands Community Land Unit, who gave the meeting an overview of other community land initiatives, including a brief résumé of the rationale behind previous buy-outs such as Assynt, Eigg, Orbost and smaller-scale purchases such as Abriachan Forest. He went on to explain the processes involved in a buy-out, and what support and funding were available from the

Community Land Unit (CLU) and from the Scottish Land Fund (SLF). He finished by pointing out some of the potential benefits of community landownership, such as 'developing new homes or making sites available for affordable housing, stemming the out-migration of families and attracting new families to the area through creation of job opportunities and generally raising confidence in the future through an active development strategy.' (HIE, *Community Land Ownership*, p.7.)

Simon Fraser, a lawyer in Stornoway and a much-respected veteran of community buy-outs since the historic buy-out of the Assynt estate in 1992, was next to speak. Assuring his audience that he represented no particular interest group, Simon Fraser advised those present to be open-minded about their options from the outset and to take full advantage of the professional support available.

Opening a more general discussion, Alasdair Morrison invited both Councillors to give their views on the implications of the sale of Amhuinnsuidhe Estate. The Councillor for Harris East, Donald MacDonald, seems to have been typical of many of those who had just begun to absorb the news. He felt that while Harris was certainly in need of regeneration, he and others needed more time to take in all the implications both of the sale and of any kind of buy-out. Councillor Morag Munro (Harris West) made the crucial point that the estate included both crofting and non-crofting interests and that, as there were so few people present, another meeting with a wider representation of the community would be needed. Although she agreed with Councillor MacDonald that caution was needed and that the Estate had liabilities as well as assets, she firmly believed that the sale could provide a real opportunity for Harris.

Interestingly, the general public preferred to listen to the speakers rather than participate in the discussion. Those who did contribute did so in response to an invitation from the Chair, or because they were representing views put to them by people who were themselves reluctant to speak. One reflection of such views was articulated by John Murdo Morrison of The Harris Hotel, a prominent and well-respected businessman in Harris. Never afraid to be forthright in expressing an opinion, John

Murdo Morrison voiced his serious doubts as to the viability of any buy-out which involved the Castle. From his own experience of Harris Hotel, which dated from 1865, he was well aware of the problems associated with maintaining an ageing building in good repair. He knew that the upkeep of Amhuinnsuidhe Castle, which dates from the same decade, would be an expensive undertaking. He pointed out that The Stornoway Trust found it almost impossible to afford the upkeep of Lews Castle, and feared that Amhuinnsuidhe Castle could become a 'millstone round the neck' of the community if they bought it. Somehow, probably because in the heat of the moment he used the words 'castles in the air,' the phrase was attributed to him in the press. Such negative comments from a well-known figure made wonderful headlines for those journalists who wanted to find melodrama and controversy in what had been in every respect a restrained and thoughtful discussion. This sensationalist picture in the press of a community rushing into an ill-considered decision was in marked contrast to remarks made at the meeting such as 'we must be realistic,' 'we have nothing to lose by looking into it,' 'communities can develop when they believe in themselves,' and 'there is a lot of potential for development in Harris.'

Perhaps the most telling argument for considering the matter further was that, although Jonathan Bulmer had been seen as a benevolent landowner, there was no guarantee that a new owner would be the same. On the question of a community-owned estate generating enough revenue to make a community buy-out a viable enterprise, the advice from John Watt of the Community Land Fund was to speak to people in other communities where a buy-out had already taken place, and learn from their experience that there was no single model for generating financial viability.

Calum MacKay, who was later to become Chairman of the North Harris Trust, summed up the mood of the meeting: 'It is interesting and heartening that there is so much interest in the sale of the estate and what it might mean. Community ownership is one way of being sure of the future, but all the liabilities and opportunities need to be looked at.'

Three important decisions were taken at that first meeting.

There was a cautious consensus for further exploration of what a community buy-out might involve. As the relatively small number of people present was not representative of the whole community, it was decided to hold a second meeting in the hope of involving a larger number of people. Finally, in order to examine all the implications of the community buying the estate, a Steering Group was elected. In the first instance, the North Harris Community Steering Group was a sub-group of Harris Development Ltd. (HDL). Kenny Mackay, Chairman of HDL, was appointed as acting Chair of the group, and Duncan MacPherson of HDL was asked to supply secretarial support. The first members elected to the Steering Group were David Cameron, a businessman in Tarbert; Steve McCombe, a crofter, but resident in Tarbert; Ronnie Morrison, a retired banker; Councillor Morag Munro; Calum Mackay, a teacher, and Barbara Mackay, also a teacher.

After the public meeting, a somewhat shell-shocked Steering Group held what was to be the first of many meetings. Their remit was to collect information about the estate, investigate the feasibility of buying it, and report back to the wider community on their findings. Conscious that the press would be on the phone to each and every member of the group at the earliest opportunity, it was agreed that Councillor Morag Munro would be spokesperson for the Steering Group. This sophisticated and well-co-ordinated approach to the media was to serve them well throughout the life of the Steering Group. Duncan MacPherson was asked to write to Jonathan Bulmer and his selling agent, formally notifying them of the community's interest, and to apply to the Community Land Unit for a start-up grant. A second meeting was arranged for 13 May 2002, and guest speakers were to be invited from the communities of Assynt and Valtos, where community buy-outs had already taken place. Finally, a report of the first meeting and details of the second meeting were to be sent to the local newsletter *Dé Tha Dol?*

After the meeting, Duncan MacPherson drove Kenny Mackay home along the winding road to Rhenigidale. The question uppermost in the minds of both men was, 'What have we got ourselves into?' Over the following months they were to learn that the answer to that question was meetings, meetings and more meetings, and eventually the purchase of the North Harris Estate.

Chapter 2
The North Harris Community Steering Group

The boundaries and full particulars of what the Amhuinnsuidhe Estate comprised had not been available to the meeting on 29 April and would not be available until well into May. In order to get a feel for the area while they were in Harris, John Watt and Sandra Holmes of Highlands and Islands Enterprise took a trip around the Estate the day after the first public meeting, and met some of the people with whom they might be working if a buy-out went ahead. Incidentally, it is worth recording that the presence of these representatives of Highlands and Islands Enterprise in Harris for a couple of days was in marked contrast to the preference of representatives from the old Highlands and Islands Development Board for Island people to present themselves for meetings, at least in Stornoway, if not in Inverness. On this very brief inspection John Watt and Sandra Holmes concluded that, although the land was marginal and predominantly rocky moorland, the Estate had substantial assets in the castle, excellent fishings and spectacular scenery. The fact that the owner had invested significant money in the estate, that he enjoyed a good relationship with the local community and was willing to discuss the sale with community representatives, were positive factors.

Both Sandra Holmes and John Watt realised that it was difficult to assess the response of the community at large from the reaction of the relatively small number of people who had been present at the public meeting the previous evening. They were also conscious of the fact that the Estate would be advertised on the open market with a daunting price tag of £4.5m. As North Harris was a high quality sporting estate, a community buy-out using significant amounts of public money would be keenly scrutinised and fiercely criticised by the Scottish Landowners' Federation and by other landowner interest groups. Newspaper headlines such as 'Public money for community to buy lavish mansion' were not difficult to envisage. While the perception was intangible, it might also have been important that the estate did not have the romanticism and strong community identity which had fired the public imagination in the buy-outs of Assynt and Eigg. Major problems to be considered were the economics of running the estate, whether it would be necessary to buy all the estate assets, and the possibly adverse effect on the value and potential use of the sporting rights if the Castle were to be split from the remainder of the estate.

Before any real progress could be made in exploring the possibility of a community buy-out, the North Harris Community Steering Group would have to apply for, and be awarded, a start-up grant. In order to assess the pros and cons of a community buy-out, a feasibility study by rural land specialists would be needed. It was to provide funding and assistance with these tasks that the Community Land Unit been established. Both John Watt and Sandra Holmes were to play a vital role in providing the day-to-day guidance and support which the Steering Group would need.

In 1997 Highlands and Islands Enterprise, which was the principal public sector development agency in Northern Scotland, had been asked by Brian Wilson MP (at the time Minister of State at the Scottish Office for Education, Industry and the Highlands and Islands) to set up a Community Land Unit. James Hunter, a recent Chairman of Highlands and Islands Enterprise, describing this initiative in 1999, said,

> 'From an HIE perspective ... community land ownership is not so much an end in itself, more a means to attaining the wider economic and social development of the Highlands and Islands. At the centre of such development has to be the enhancement of collective self-confidence in rural communities which, until recently, had virtually no prospect of ever having any worthwhile say in the management of one of their most basic assets – their land.' (James Hunter in J. McAskill, We have won the Land, 1999, p. 9.)

The climate of opinion in favour of community landownership

had been gaining momentum from at least the late 1980s. The purchase of the Assynt Estate in 1992 had broken the mould, and this was followed by a series of acquisitions such as Eigg, Bhaltos, Knoydart, Gigha and Melness – each of them distinctive, and none of them exactly like the North Harris Estate. Nonetheless, these places did have features in common with North Harris and these coincided with the aims of the Community Land Unit.

The most urgent of these features were rural depopulation (the population of Harris had dropped by over 11% from 2,240 in 1991 to 1,984 in 2001) and the consequent loss of viability within the crofting community. Examples of this kind of loss of viability include situations in which an ageing population can no longer participate in communal tasks such as the gathering and fanking of sheep; a fragile economic base dependent on the vagaries of tourism, fish farming and fish processing; and, as Sandra Holmes described it after the first public meeting, 'a spectacular, but vulnerable natural environment' threatened, for example, by the possibility of oil spills in the Minch or industrial-scale quarrying. While no-one would claim that community land ownership is a panacea for all the problems of a community in decline, the experience and achievements of communities such as Assynt, Eigg and Gigha, to name but three, went to show that when communities are 'put in the driving seat they can steer a course towards future development that is geared specifically towards the needs and particular characteristics of their own community.' (HIE, *Community Landownership*.)

Specifically, the North Harris community could at least hope that ownership of the land would enable them to stem the tide of out-migration of young families, and to attract new families to the area by creating suitable employment opportunities – by creating jobs associated with the estate and by providing workshop and office space for new enterprises. They could hope to make plots available to provide affordable housing and to re-furbish derelict estate property. They could hope to facilitate new employment initiatives by enhancing and conserving the natural environment, thereby qualifying for grants through agreements with such agencies as Scottish National Heritage and similar bodies. Such activities all matched the criteria envisaged within the Community Land Unit remit.

Many of the funding problems which challenged the people of Assynt in 1992-93 had been resolved by the time the North Harris Estate came on the market. The organisational structure through which land acquisitions could be made at the time is complicated for the layman to understand. John Watt of Highlands and Islands Enterprise took the trouble to provide the writer with a helpful explanation of that structure.

> *'The Lottery, at that time had a range of funds, one of which was the New Opportunities Fund. Within this fund there was a range of programmes, one of which was the Green Spaces and Sustainable Communities Programme. A sub-set of the Green Spaces and Sustainable Communities programme was the Scottish Land Fund which operated specifically in Scotland to assist communities to acquire land and property. Prior to the establishment of the Scottish Land Fund, the only public money available for communities to acquire land was from Highlands and Islands Enterprise. This was not a large fund. When the Scottish Land Fund came into operation in 2001, it became the 'first brick in the wall' for community acquisitions. The Lottery's New Opportunities Fund chose Highlands and Islands Enterprise to administer and deliver this fund on its behalf across the whole of Scotland. The Community Land Unit was a special team set up within Highlands and Islands Enterprise, specifically to deliver community land ownership objectives and to administer the Scottish Land Fund.'* (John Watt, letter to NHT, 08 December, 2006.)

Introducing the Scottish Land Fund, Jill Pitkeathley OBE, Chair of the New Opportunities Fund, wrote: 'The New Opportunities Fund chose Highlands and Islands Enterprise and Scottish Enterprise to become Award Partners under our Green Spaces and

Sustainable Communities programme, to ensure that funding is available to help communities acquire, develop and manage local land and land assets. The Highlands and Islands Enterprise and Scottish Enterprise partnership was selected because it was well placed to effect real change in achieving a more sustainable future for rural communities throughout Scotland.' (HIE, *The Scottish Land Fund: Ionmhas Fearainn na h-Alba.)* When Highlands and Islands Enterprise was appointed to administer the Scottish Land Fund, they expanded the Community Land Unit and, in keeping with their commitment to decentralisation, established the main Scottish Land Fund (SLF) office in Auchtertyre, near Kyle of Lochalsh. Sandra Holmes worked from that office in Auchtertyre.

In the months leading to the buy-out of the North Harris Estate, Sandra Holmes was involved on an almost daily basis with the North Harris Community Steering Group. Apart from members of the Steering Group, the other person involved on a day-to-day basis with the practical detail of the buy-out was Duncan MacPherson of Harris Development Ltd, who agreed at the first meeting to be responsible for supplying secretarial support to the Steering Group. Harris Development Ltd. (HDL) is a community-led development company created in 1994. It arose out of concern about the economic and demographic decline that was becoming obvious in Harris in the early 1990s. It was formed by a partnership between Comhairle nan Eilean Siar, Western Isles Enterprise, Western Isles Tourist Board, the Harris Community Councils, voluntary organisations and six local people. There were two hundred members. Among the HDL projects were the Scaladale Centre, Seallam Genealogical Centre and the MacGillivray Centre at Northton, the land infill in the bay at Tarbert, the traditional boat-building centre at Flodabay and the Harris Walkway. All these projects have contributed to a new sense of purpose and achievement in Harris.

The existence of Harris Development Ltd from 1994 and the number of projects successfully initiated by it were ample proof that here was a community doing its best to help itself. In April 2002, the people of North Harris were faced with the choice of whether or not to take a potentially more effective step towards influencing their own future, with the decision to explore the possibility of buying the land on which they lived.

Chapter 3
A Decisive Meeting

Over the two weeks following the meeting on Monday 29 April, the North Harris Community Steering Group (NHCSG) began to get a foretaste of what the months ahead would be like. It was to be a summer and autumn of frequent meetings, sometimes as many as two per week. In the run-up to the ballot, meetings were held daily. Sandra Holmes (CLU) had drafted a list of the steps which would have to be taken. These included the Steering Group making application to the Community Land Unit for a start-up grant, and arranging a second and more representative Public Meeting through the community newspaper *Dé tha Dol?* Duncan MacPherson of Harris Development Ltd., as acting Secretary to the Steering Group, had to write formally to Jonathan Bulmer and his selling agent to register the interest of the community in buying the Estate. Then they had to arrange a meeting with Jonathan Bulmer to discuss the sale. A technical aid team had to be set up to be ready to assist the community if it decided to pursue the option of a buy-out of the Estate.

For the population of the scattered villages in North Harris, attending a meeting in Tarbert is much more than a mere five or ten-minute journey by car. While the road over the Clisham from the North Harris boundary to Tarbert has been greatly improved, even on this road there were, in 2002, still sizeable sections which were single track with passing places. Unless one is a driving connoisseur who enjoys the challenge of switchback bends and reversing to the last passing place on a single track road with the constant hazard of wandering sheep, driving along the Amhuinnsuidhe peninsula from Govig or Hushinish to Tarbert can be a challenge, especially in the dark or in wind and rain. Though only fifteen miles, the journey takes a good half-hour, probably forty minutes for a careful driver, depending on the amount of oncoming traffic. In the other direction, driving approximately twelve miles to Rhenigidale over another narrow, twisting, switchback road takes almost twice as long as the same distance would on a mainland road; the road from Kyles Scalpay to Tarbert is only marginally better.

No less than four meetings took place on Monday 13 May. In the afternoon the Acting Chairman, Kenny MacKay (Rhenigidale), John Watt (CLU) and Sandra Homes (SLF) met with Jonathan Bulmer, his son Sebastian Bulmer, and the Estate Factor, George Macdonald. The discussion was amicable and informative. John Watt stressed that the community would need the maximum amount of information on the Estate and its finances. They would also need time to assimilate this information and, if they decided to go ahead with further exploration of the project, they would need time to have a Feasibility Study prepared. Jonathan Bulmer was very willing to supply all information that was needed and expressed his own sympathy with the aspirations of the North Harris community.

It became clear from the discussion that the Estate was owned by a Trust whose beneficiaries were the Bulmer family. This Trust had therefore a duty to maximise the value of the Estate for the benefit of that family. There were twenty-five estate employees, five of whom were permanent and full-time, and the estate had a turnover of approximately £400,000 per annum, which allowed it to break even. The hatchery was on an annual lease, and there was no income from the Hydro-Electric power station. A copy of the fisheries returns and a copy of the application form for the Ranger Service were supplied and both of these documents contained a lot of useful information.

The next three meetings were all in the evening of Monday 13 May and were held in the Community Centre in Tarbert. These were: a preparatory meeting of the Steering Group Committee at 6.30pm, the very important Public Meeting at 8pm, and another Steering Group Committee meeting immediately after the Public Meeting.

While the information from the afternoon meeting with Jonathan Bulmer was of considerable interest to the Steering Group, the discussion at 6.30pm centred on the best way of handling the crucially important Public Meeting to come. Everyone agreed that, as the community had already voted to set up the Steering Group, there was no point in having a second vote on that issue. What was vital was that they should ask those present for a wider geographical representation on the Steering Group. Another subject for discussion was the matter of arranging for a Feasibility Study. It was obvious that confidence in the firm commissioned to do the Feasibility Study would be of paramount importance. It was equally vital that the firm's assessment of the impact of a community on the local economy was reliable. While there were various firms with relevant experience, it seemed sensible that the Feasibility Study should be put out to tender. The work of the Feasibility Study would be commissioned by the North Harris Community Steering Group (NHCSG) rather than by the Community Land Unit.

In order to benefit from the experience of other communities where a buy-out had been successfully achieved, the Steering Group had invited John Mackenzie from Assynt, Sandy MacKenzie from Bhaltos, and Willie Smith of the Crofters' Commission to attend the meeting as guest speakers. Asked by David Cameron about the level of support for a community buy-out in Assynt, John Mackenzie told them that it had been 90% in favour. The vital question was, could they aspire to such overwhelming support in North Harris?

By eight o'clock on Monday 13 May, members of the Steering Group could look around the Community Centre in Tarbert and feel a sense of relief. The work they had done in encouraging people to attend the meeting had been well-rewarded. The second Public Meeting was attended by twice as many people as had been present at the first meeting in April. As is normal in the Western Isles on such a significant occasion, the meeting was opened with a prayer, on this occasion by the Rev. Norman Maciver. The Acting Chairman Kenny MacKay then assured the audience that no decision on making a bid for the estate would be taken without the consent of the community. The guest speakers were invited in turn to address the meeting. The first speaker was Alasdair Morrison MSP, who had been instrumental in calling the initial meeting at the end of April when news of the sale by Jonathan Bulmer became public knowledge.

Alasdair Morrison opened his remarks by saying that he was well aware of the concerns that his own involvement in the project might cause. He admitted that he personally was unashamedly in favour of community landownership, but was keen to reassure the audience that the decision would be taken by the community and that politicians could not, and would not, foist any decision upon them. The most important message was that it would cost the community nothing to examine the pros and cons of a buy-out, but that, if they decided not even to examine the issue, future generations might well ask why. While the HIE Community Land Unit had not been in existence when the Assynt estate was on the market, the Community Land Unit had been of great help in later buy-outs. It was Alasdair Morrison's firm belief that the unit had been an outstanding success.

A positive account of existing community buy-outs was then provided by the two guest speakers: the veteran of the first ever buy-out, John Mackenzie from Assynt, and Sandy MacKenzie from the much more recent buy-out of Bhaltos in Lewis. John Mackenzie spoke first. Expressing his appreciation of the prayer acknowledging God's sovereignty in their decision, John MacKenzie went on to give a brief history of what had occurred in what is now called The North Assynt Estate. The history of that estate provides a sad example of the frivolous attitude to landownership typified, in this instance, by the Duke of Westminster. According to local tradition, the Duke bought Assynt sometime after the First World War, as a wedding present for his son-in law, William Filmer–Sankey. Over the next few years, this owner proceeded to sell off the family silver in a series of sales to the Vestey family, starting with the coastal crofting land. Some years later, the Vesteys in their turn began further fragmentation, selling part of the estate in 1989 to Scandinavian Property Services Ltd, a company which in 1992 went into liquidation. The crofters on the estate only learned of the imminent sale of the land on which they lived and worked when some of them went to help a party of potential purchasers whose seaplane was stuck in the soft sand on Clashnessie Beach. Little wonder that curiosity arises in a rural community when exotic strangers appear on the scene. It was the prospect of further fragmentation in 1992 which proved the last straw and led eventually to the community buy-out.

In addition to the interesting details of the Assynt experience, John Mackenzie did have some advice which was particularly relevant to the situation in North Harris in May 2002. In Assynt, an encouraging Feasibility Study led to a campaign for funds. More than half of the £80,000 they required had come from crofters and their supporters. They had been greatly helped by favourable press coverage. At the third attempt, they managed to buy the estate for £300,000. A decisive factor in their campaign had been their formidable opposition to other buyers, in particular their resistance to the sale of the salmon fishing and the lodge. It is worth noting that in Assynt, unlike North Harris, almost all the acreage of the estate was in crofting. Therefore, in Assynt, the threat of individual crofters deciding to exercise their right to buy their individual crofts under the 1976 Act had been a powerful weapon in the struggle to buy the estate.

Looking back at what had been achieved in the nine years since the buy-out of the North Assynt Estate, John Mackenzie told the audience that virtually every township had started a woodland project averaging 100 hectares, and these woods had attracted £90-£100,000 of funding; the woodlands were capable of generating £6000 per annum per township. He said that, as the North Assynt Estate was an easily identifiable area, universities had shown an interest in projects there. Renewable energy had been the most ambitious project, and a small Hydro-Electric scheme was producing an income of approximately £1,600 per week. The capital cost of this scheme had been in excess of £500,000, with grant assistance almost equivalent to the purchase price of the estate. The Estate received 5.4p per unit of electricity and would be clear of debt in ten years. For the next five years, £200,000 would be shared between the Estate and a partner. The scheme would continue to produce income for fifty years with all the money going to the Estate. This income would be used to generate business opportunities for young people in the area. He admitted that, although there was no landlord for people to criticise and while there had been disagreements, the democratic vote prevailed. When John Mackenzie stopped speaking, there was a moment's silence and then spontaneous applause broke out around the hall. Looking back at that moment, Duncan MacPherson would say that it was the turning point, the moment when doubt, even antipathy, turned to conviction, even enthusiasm, for the buy-out.

Sandy MacKenzie of Bhaltos was invited to speak next. He explained that Bhaltos, a much smaller and more recently-acquired estate which had been parcelled off from the larger Uig and Hamnaway Estate, was only 700 hectares. It had been a very different type of buy-out. For instance, the estate had not been placed on the open market. The situation in Bhaltos had few features in common with North Harris, apart from the principle of the people in the community deciding to take responsibility for the land they lived on. As Sandy MacKenzie told the audience, had they not decided to buy the land when it was on the market, they might have got a good landlord and possibly they might not.

As it was important for everyone attending the meeting to have an understanding of what exactly community land ownership was and how it applied to North Harris before the meeting was opened to general discussion and questions from the floor, John Watt of Highlands and Islands Enterprise (HIE) Community Land Unit (CLU) was invited to speak. Explaining why a community might want to buy the land, John Watt said that some communities wanted to bring stability to local landownership, as this could help to protect jobs and investments. It could also enable communities to identify and exploit further development opportunities. The most workable model of Community Landownership was for the community to form a company. People could then apply to become members of that company. The company would be run by a Board of Directors, formally elected by the members, and in many cases it would be registered as a charity. It was vital to establish if it was feasible for the community to buy the estate. The community would need to look carefully at the issue with the help of the CLU and with other professional assistance. Once detailed information had been collected, the community and CLU could look at options for running the estate in the future. John Watt, speaking from wide experience of earlier community buy-outs, emphasised that one cost to the community would be time – a warning which in the event was to be all too true.

He went on to explain that, if they decided to examine the possibility of a community buy-out, and before a report on the various options was made available, it would be wise for them to go and look at other communities where a buy-out had been accomplished. Turning specifically to the topic of North Harris, he said that the purchase could be carried out alone, or with a partner. The community might wish to have a ballot before going ahead. If they did hold a ballot, and did decide to continue with a buy-out, the Steering Group would then stand down and a new committee would be elected.

On the question of what financial assistance would be available, John Watt told the meeting that a start-up grant of £2000 was already on its way to the North Harris Community Steering Group. Further assistance would also be available to commission experts to carry out studies.

If, in due course, the decision was to go ahead with a buy-out and a compelling case could be made, the Scottish Land Fund (SLF) could potentially pay up to 75% of the total cost of the land purchase, with HIE contributing 75% of the balance. This would leave the community to pay a minimum of 6% which, in the case of North Harris would be in excess of £200,000. Normal limits to funding were £1 million from the Scottish Land Fund (SLF) and £250,000 from HIE. However, in Gigha, the SLF gave £3.5 million and HIE gave £0.5 million, with the community having to repay £1million of the SLF grant back to the Lottery within 2 years.

Before any money was given, the funding bodies had to be convinced of two things:

1. That there was strong community support, and
2. That there was a strong business case.

John Watt went on to say that assistance could continue after the purchase had been made, with funds being made available for investment and the employment of a manager. An aftercare officer would be made available to provide on-going support to the Board in the post-acquisition stage, and HIE could appoint a Director to the Board if that appeared to be appropriate. Answering the anticipated question, 'Who does the buy-out?' John Watt said that the community did, with considerable assistance from various agencies. (NHCSG Minute of Public Meeting of 13 May 2002, at 8pm.)

At this point, the Chairman Kenny Mackay thanked the guest speakers for their contributions, and opened the meeting to questions from the floor. The range of questions revealed that people had a number of concerns about the implications of a buy-out. As if he feared that events were moving too quickly, Councillor Donald Macdonald said that he would want to see a ballot before there was any decision to go ahead. He voiced his concerns about the timescale, the amount of work involved in a buy-out, and about the views of older people who were unable to come to a public meeting. He also felt the need for an enlarged committee, and thought that it would be advisable to have people on the committee who were opposed to the buy-out. Councillor Macdonald was less apprehensive when he was told that those on the Steering Group were not necessarily committed to a buy-out, but simply wanted to look at the situation, and when the results of a feasibility study had been made available a ballot of the community would take place.

In view of what had been said about the financing of the Gigha buy-out, John Mitchell asked a number of questions about what might happen in Harris. The most important of these questions was, 'What is the assistance regarding capital and running costs, as it is more important to focus on the running costs of an estate?' John Watt replied that the running costs were absolutely fundamental and would be at the core of the business planning. He said, 'There is the potential for the community to work with a commercial partner or to lease out some element of the estate to a private operator. Community companies can also access funds such as charitable trusts.' (NHCSG Minute of Public Meeting, 13 May 2003 at 8pm, p.4.)

Despite what he had heard in the course of the meeting, John Murdo Morrison, a local businessman who had just retired as owner of the Harris Hotel in Tarbert, was still not convinced.

He said that he felt duty-bound to express his doubts about the buy-out. In his opinion, there was no comparison between North Harris and Gigha, Eigg and Bhaltos, in that North Harris was much larger, with a number of diverse townships and with the town of Tarbert. He wanted to know who would have a vote. Would it be only crofters, or would newcomers to the community have a vote? He felt that members of the community were being used as pawns in a political game. Alasdair Morrison MSP replied that the questions which John Murdo Morrison had asked reinforced the need for a Feasibility Study. Those eligible to vote would include anyone on the Electoral Roll who lived within the boundary of the estate. He assured him that people would be voting on facts, and that although Jonathan Bulmer had been a good landlord, there was no certainty that any new private landowner would be like him. The MSP believed that the community now had to look to the future. Personally, he wanted to see sustained economic development for all parts of the Western Isles, including North Harris.

Among the topics raised, there was a degree of concern that the rights of crofters would somehow be affected by a community buy-out. Alasdair Morrison MSP reassured the meeting that those rights would be unaffected and would remain as strong as ever. Councillor MacDonald enquired about the mineral rights, and John Watt replied that these could be bought if they were being sold with the land. Referring to the previous question, he went on to say that any group applying for public funding must have an open membership. A 'crofters-only' group would not be eligible for SLF and HIE funding. Another question asked was whether the community would be burdened with paying back borrowings. It is worth noting here that funding from SLF and CLU was in the form of a grant, not a loan. John Watt replied to the questioner saying that very few communities had had borrowings. Bhaltos did not have any borrowings, and although Assynt did borrow £100,000, they had subsequently repaid this. However, it was unlikely that the SLF would approve assistance to any projects which were unable to generate enough income to service their loan finance, if a loan were made. (NHCSG Minute of Public Meeting of 13 May 2002, at 8pm.)

At 10.30 pm, immediately after the Public Meeting, the Steering Group, with the addition of two new members, Donald MacLennan (Govig) and Duncan MacLeod (Urgha) met to plan the way ahead. Discussion centred on the mechanics of setting a Feasibility Study in motion. John Watt promised to send members a brief for potential consultants so that they could amend it as they saw fit. Calum MacKay took on responsibility for writing articles for the press, and Councillor Morag Munro agreed to be spokesperson for the group. An update of events would be published in *Dé Tha Dol?* every fortnight.

The variety and detail of the questions asked at the public meeting, and the inherent caution, even healthy scepticism, displayed by many of those present, confound any suggestion that the people of North Harris rushed unthinkingly into the process of buying the land on which they lived and worked. Certainly they were not carried away by romantic optimism, nor were they in anyway political pawns – far from it. Their decision to investigate the economic and social implications of a buy-out through the mechanism of a Feasibility Study was driven neither by anti-landlordism, nor yet by 'fashionable bandwagon-jumping,' as was alleged by one journalist (Écosse, *Sunday Times*, 15 September 2002) but by a sense of responsibility for the future of their children and the land on which their livelihoods depended. A strong belief in the value of exploring the possibility of a buy-out, tempered by caution and down-to earth realism, seem to have been the prevailing emotions as they went home that night.

Chapter 4
A Busy Summer

The members of the North Harris Community Steering
Group who met on 17 May 2002 to begin the process of
commissioning a Feasibility Study for a potential buy-out of the
estate could have been forgiven if they were somewhat daunted
by the enormity of the task which lay ahead of them. Crofters,
teachers and local businessmen, they had little experience of
the complexities of the land market. Their confidence would
not have been helped by a somewhat tongue-in-cheek account
of the public meeting of 13 May by a local reporter writing as
an 'insider,' which had been published in the *Weekend Herald
Magazine*. (*Weekend Herald Magazine, 25.05 02.*) That at least
some of their friends and neighbours in North Harris certainly
saw the whole project as ill-advised would not have made their
task any easier. Without the guidance and expertise of Sandra
Holmes and John Watt of the Community Land Unit, the ever-
available advice of Simon Fraser, the lawyer who had guided
so many other community buy-outs, their courage might have
failed them. The level-headed and competent presence of Duncan
MacPherson, seconded from Harris Development Ltd to provide
secretarial help to the Steering Group, did much to facilitate
the almost daily contact between the Steering Group and the
Community Land Unit.

In the broadest terms, their responsibilities over the early
summer involved preparing a brief for the Feasibility Study
and then putting that finalised brief out to tender. They had
to decide on a number of consultants to receive the brief, and
when tenders had been submitted, to select the most suitable
firm of consultants to undertake the task. When a Feasibility
Study had eventually been submitted, the Group had the most
important responsibility of deciding whether to recommend to
the community that it was possible to go ahead and bid for the
estate, or part of it, or that they should turn their backs on the
whole idea. At the same time, they had to apply for funding for
the Feasibility Study and commission an independent valuation

of the assets of the estate. Once the estate had been advertised on the open market with full details of the assets to be sold and a firm asking price known, they had to be aware of competition from other potential buyers and react appropriately to press interest. Time was not on their side. Although Jonathan Bulmer had indicated that the actual sale might not take place until the autumn and that he looked sympathetically on the community's aspirations to buy the estate, there was always the fear that if a satisfactory bid was made by somebody in the interim, they might lose the chance to buy. Above all it was vital to retain the goodwill of the community by keeping them informed as to what was happening.

A discussion paper prepared by David Cameron allowed the Steering Group to agree from the outset on strategies and individual responsibilities. Everyone on the Steering Group was agreed that they wanted a Feasibility Study, that they wanted to keep an open mind as to the eventual decision, and that there should be no financial cost to the community in conducting the Feasibility Study. Calum MacKay accepted the responsibility of writing fortnightly articles for the community newsletter *Dé tha Dol?* and also agreed to write a flyer which would be sent to every home in North Harris to inform people when consultants had been appointed to undertake a Feasibility Study. Advice would be taken from Simon Fraser as to what percentage of the community voting in favour of a buy-out would be required to allow a bid to be made for the estate. All communications would be approved by the Chair and Vice-Chair of the Steering Group. If the committee were to split on an issue, the Chair would have the casting vote. There were other relatively minor decisions to be taken, and one of these sheds a revealing light on the tactful – but determined – independence of mind shown by the Steering Group. It was decided that from then on, politicians would be kept at arm's length. The Chair, Kenny Mackay, would write to Alasdair Morrison MSP to thank him for his assistance thus far and to inform him that the committee would advise him of progress. Having cleared the decks, they turned their minds to the urgent task of examining the draft brief prepared by John Watt (CLU) for a Feasibility Study.

The purpose of the Feasibility Study was to assist the community in identifying the economic, social and environmental development potential of the estate and the feasibility of various development options. In mid-May the Steering Group discussed this draft brief paragraph by paragraph and made a few minor changes to it. The potential consultants were given a short account of events which had taken place since the estate had gone on the market at the end of April. Although the full particulars of the estate would not be available until the end of May 2002, it was possible for the brief to provide the consultants with a reasonable amount of information as to what the community might want to buy.

The Brief for Consultants described the estate thus:

> 'The estate comprises approximately 50,000 acres of which approximately 20,000 acres are under crofting tenure. There are 12 crofting townships and 104 crofts. The estate is primarily used for sporting activities, boasting some of the best stalking and fishing in the Western Isles and indeed in the Highlands and Islands. The most recent catches included 14 stags, 212 salmon and 490 sea trout. These figures perform above average and compare with declines seen in many other areas. A considerable proportion of the estate (over 50%) is covered by natural heritage designations such as SSSI, SAC and SPA.

> The estate also includes Amhuinnsuidhe Castle. This building was constructed in classic Victorian style in 1867, and has been refurbished to a high standard. It is used as the base for stalking and fishing activities. In addition, in an attempt to diversify the estate's income generation potential, cookery, photography and painting holidays take place in the Castle. These are aimed at the top end of the market, starting at £1,000 per person per week for a fully catered and

instructed holiday. There are also several smaller properties adjoining the castle and elsewhere on the estate in varying states of repair. Accounts for the last two years of the estate's activities will be provided to the successful consultant. Current turnover is c. £400,000.

There is a range of ownership scenarios facing the community. The viability of these is significantly influenced by:

- The funding package which would be required for the community to acquire the whole estate or significant parts of it
- The ability to generate income depending on which assets the community decides, or is able, to acquire.

Various ownership scenarios can be envisaged therefore:

- all assets acquired and retained by the community
- all assets acquired and some leased or sold to commercial operators
- only some assets acquired e.g. land under crofting tenure, with others acquired by other commercial interests, either arm's length or in partnership with the community.

Objectives of the Study

1. The study has the following primary objectives: Analysis of the current income and expenditure pattern of the estate.
2. In consultation with the community, collating and assessing ideas for development opportunities that could arise if the estate was in community ownership.

These could involve sporting, environmental, business, renewable energy and tourism activities, together with provision of infrastructure including land for other economic activities and housing.
3. Preparation of annual income and expenditure projections bearing in mind development opportunities, and various ownership scenarios described above.
4. An analysis of options for raising funds.
5. An assessment of the economic impact of selected scenarios, both at the local (Harris) and wider Western Isles levels.

Expected Outcomes

1. An opinion on the medium to long-term viability of the existing estate activities.
2. Proposals on developing new enterprises/activities.
3. A series of options on running the Estate in the light of the potential ownership scenarios listed above.
4. Recommendations on the viability of each possible option of operating the existing business, with a prioritised list of future options which should be considered to strengthen overall viability.
5. A recommendation on the viability of the community purchasing and operating the Estate.'

(Extract from North Harris Steering Group Brief for Consultants, 20 May 2002.)

This brief was then sent out to seven companies of consultants, all of whom had experience of the sort of research and investigation needed for community buy-outs.

Out of the seven companies which had received copies of the Brief for Consultants, only three submitted tenders. At the meeting of the Steering Group on 4 June, a joint consultation took place between the Steering Group in Tarbert and John Watt in Inverness via a videolink. The most important criteria which influenced the choice of the Steering Group were the attention to be paid to consulting with the local community, and the thoroughness of the consultant's assessment of the economic impact of a potential buy-out. The decision was difficult. Eventually, the meeting agreed to invite representatives of each of the three companies to Harris for interview by a panel of four members of the Group. Any sighs of relief at resolving that dilemma were slightly premature when they were reminded that they could not appoint a consultant until funds had been approved by Highlands and Islands Enterprise and the Scottish Land Fund. That application for funding was the next hurdle to be tackled. While the man in the street can be forgiven for making a mess of filling in even the simplest of forms, this application for funding for the Feasibility Study was one form which had to be filled in without mistakes. Calum Mackay was therefore glad to have the expertise of Sandra Holmes (CLU) to advise him about completing the application form. (Minutes of NHCSG Meeting 04 June 2002 and 11 June 2002.)

All three sets of consultants came to Harris to be interviewed, and considerable thought and care went into choosing who would be awarded the contract. In the final analysis, the tender from Graeme Scott and Co. was considered to offer the 'best team and ethos.' Their tender had 'a strong financial/economic input.' The team included an expert on marine-related issues, a member with knowledge of estate management issues, and a member in the hotel sector. These points weighed in their favour, but above all they 'already had considerable experience of community buy-outs and appeared to have community participation at the very heart of their way of working.' All these points enabled the Group to reach a unanimous decision to offer them the contract. (NHCSG Minute 11 June 2002.)

It had been agreed from the beginning of the project that the remit for the North Harris Community Steering Group was to investigate the options available to the people of North Harris and, having done a Feasibility Study, to present the recommendations on these options to the community at large.

A ballot would then be held and, if the community decision was to go ahead and make a bid for the estate, the Steering Group would resign in favour of a newly-formed Community Company which would, in the name of the community, bid for and hope to buy the estate, or those parts of it they wished to acquire.

All members of the Steering Group were well aware of the pressure they were under. If the Feasibility Study should recommend that the community should go ahead with a buy-out, events would move very quickly. It was therefore important for the Group to take legal advice on the formation of a Community Company. Sandra Holmes (SLF), who was present at this meeting, told them that the charges for the legal work to set up such a company normally came out of the start-up budget and that they should get quotations for this work as soon as possible. The Group also wanted advice on the voting rights of people who worked crofts on the North Harris estate but did not live there, and on the rights, if any, of people who lived on land in North Harris which had been sold by the estate. This last group of people were those living in the Maaraig to Rhenigidale area, a section of the estate originally part of the North Harris Estate but retained by Mrs Panchaud when the Bulmers bought the estate.

From conversations with friends and neighbours in North Harris, members of the Steering Group were becoming aware of a number of preconceived attitudes and misconceptions regarding a potential buy-out. There was a belief that Highland Estates did not pay, but would lumber the community with a heavy burden of debt which would be impossible to repay, when in fact 94% of the cost might be paid by grants. Again, most people thought of and discussed the Estate solely in terms of the Castle and its immediate environs, without considering the assets of other parts of the Estate. As the eventual decision to go ahead with a buy-out or reject the whole idea depended on the reaction of the community to the recommendations in the Feasibility Study, the Steering Group were concerned that such misconceptions might prevent people from giving the Study serious consideration. A 'Question and Answer' sheet that addressed the concerns most frequently voiced was prepared by Barbara Mackay and Morag

Munro, and this was included in *Dé Tha Dol?*

The Steering Group felt that one large public meeting with the Consultants would not be enough, and that a series of meetings in different areas and with different groups of people would be needed in order to reflect the aspirations of as many people as possible. The opportunity for individuals to discuss their ideas by phone calls to members of the Group was also made available. After careful planning, a news release informing the community about the appointment of Graeme Scott and Co. as the Feasibility Study Consultants and the arrangements for meetings and phone call contacts was circulated to every household and released to the press. It read as follows:

NORTH HARRIS COMMUNITY STEERING GROUP

NEWS RELEASE

The NHCSG is pleased to announce the choice of a firm to carry out a Feasibility Study into the viability of a community purchase of the North Harris Estate.

After consideration of the merits of a number of tenders received, it was agreed that a team led by Graeme Scott & Co. should be invited to undertake the work. The process for formally appointing the consultants is currently underway. The team has considerable experience of this type of work, having been involved in Assynt, Eigg & Knoydart amongst others, and the Steering Group look forward to working with the consultants over the coming weeks.

The Feasibility Study will be very comprehensive and will focus principally on:

- An assessment of the current assets of the estate
- An analysis of the trading figures currently available for the estate
- Extensive consultation with the local community and with interested parties
- An evaluation of development opportunities on the estate
- Projected financial scenarios for the next three/five years

It will include a recommendation on whether or not community buy-out is viable in the long term.

An important part of the Feasibility Study will be the element of community consultation. It is important that the views of the local community are seriously considered within the Feasibility Study. The community consultation will therefore include focussed local meetings, interviews with community organisations, discussions with individuals within the community and discussions with interested parties out with the community.

Meetings have been arranged for interested members of the local community to meet with the team and discuss the development potential of the Estate. These are:

Tues 18th June Tarbert Community Centre 8pm
Wed 19th June Tarbert Community Centre 8pm
Cliasmol School 8pm

It is also hoped that members of the NHSCG will visit Knoydart within the next few weeks to see for themselves the effect of community ownership. This will give the NHSCG an important insight into the potential opportunities and the possible pitfalls which may lie ahead.

The Group would also like to express its gratitude for the co-operation it has received so far from Jonathan

Bulmer and the selling agents Knight Frank in responding positively to its enquiries.

The following people are available for interview: Morag Munro and Kenny MacKay.

With this momentous step, the stage was set for the crucial Feasibility Study. On its outcome depended the attitude of both the Steering Group and the people of North Harris to the possibility of bidding to buy the Estate.

Chapter 5
The Feasibility Study

It would be difficult to exaggerate the importance of the Feasibility Study. At the Public Meeting in Tarbert, when it was agreed to explore the possibility of a Community Buy-out, John Watt of the Community Land Unit said to those present,

> 'Establishing the feasibility of a purchase is vital. The community needs to look carefully at the issue with the Community Land Unit and professional assistance. Once we have detailed information we can look at options for running it in the future... Before any money is given, the funding bodies have to be convinced of two things: That there is strong community support and that there is a strong business case.' (Minute of NHCSG Public Meeting, 8pm, 13 May 2002)

That advice was reflected in the brief sent out to the Consultants and published in the flyer to the community. The Brief said:

> 'The Feasibility Study will be very comprehensive and will focus principally on:
>
> - An assessment of the current assets of the estate
> - An analysis of the trading figures currently available for the estate
> - Extensive consultation with the local community and with interested parties
> - An evaluation of development opportunities on the estate
> - Projected financial scenarios for the next three/five years
>
> It will include a recommendation on whether or not a community buy-out is viable in the long term.

An important part of the Feasibility Study will be the element of community consultation.'
(NHCSG Brief for Consultants, 20 May 2002.)

The Feasibility Consultants, Graeme Scott & Co, a team which had already been involved in the buy-outs of Assynt, Eigg & Knoydart, had two inter-dependent tasks in which their expertise, combined with the local knowledge of the Steering Group, were vital. These tasks were to create a sound business plan in order to make a viable case for funding and, while doing so, to keep the community positively involved.

It would be easy to think at a superficial glance that, apart from the castle, North Harris had little to offer as a business venture, except perhaps its spectacular scenery. Such a conclusion would be a serious underestimate of the assets of the Estate, as the Consultancy Team were to demonstrate in the Feasibility Study. There is no doubt that the presence of the Castle tended to dominate every discussion about the Estate. Having listened to serious concerns about the upkeep of Amhuinnsuidhe Castle and its associated buildings in terms of 'millstones round our necks,' the Steering Group knew very well that it would be impossible to create favourable attitudes in the community without a sound business plan which took into account the problems of the Castle. John Murdo Morrison had spoken quite bluntly about the maintenance difficulties associated with Harris Hotel, which had been built at much the same time as the Castle. Similar problems, but on a much larger, and therefore more expensive scale, were inevitable in Amhuinnsuidhe Castle. While Jonathan Bulmer used the castle both as his family home and as an upmarket hotel offering residential photography, painting and cookery courses to an exclusive and wealthy clientele, it seemed unlikely that a community trust could hope to access the same sort of market. Equally, people knew that further north in Lewis it was proving impossible for the Stornoway Trust to prevent Lews Castle from falling into dangerous disrepair. The Steering Group quickly realised that, above all, the function and upkeep of the Castle were the factors most likely to undermine the confidence of both the community and that of funding bodies in the viability of a buy-out.

In order to involve the community in the process from the start, Graeme Scott and the Steering Group arranged for two public meetings to be held in Tarbert Community Centre on the evenings of Tuesday 18th and Wednesday 19th June and another public meeting at Cliasmol School, also on the Wednesday evening. A separate meeting was held with crofters, to reassure those who were concerned that their traditional rights might be affected by any change in the landlord-tenant relationship with which they had been familiar for so long. As the future of the young people of North Harris had been a strong incentive in deciding to investigate the potential of a buy-out, Calum Mackay, a teacher in Sir Edward Scott School in Tarbert as well as a member of the Steering Group, arranged for Carola Bell, one of the Consultancy Team, to meet with school pupils, particularly those who had participated in the Young Enterprise Schemes.

Perhaps the most useful of all the meetings was that held with the Grazings Clerks of the North Harris crofting townships. This was the first time that the Clerks had come together as a group. They considered how best to include all townships in future discussions. They all saw crofting in its current form declining quite rapidly, as there were fewer and fewer physically able people left in the townships. The poor land meant that there were few alternatives to the traditional activities on the crofts. The Grazings Clerks identified the lack of employment as the reason why young people could no longer continue to live locally. They saw the creation of good jobs as the only way to ensure a future for crofting, and for people to live in the more remote areas. Retaining young people in North Harris was seen as the critical problem to be tackled. The effort by the Steering Group to find ways of re-invigorating crofting and to reassure crofters that their rights would stay the same under a community buy-out was seen very worthwhile. The meeting of Grazings Clerks ended with a positive feeling from those present that there was much more to be considered in regard to community ownership, and this feeling was based upon their improved understanding of some of the issues. There was a general consensus that it was very important that more information should be made available

NHT Directors & Staff:
Back row: Alistair Macleod, Calum Mackay, Mick Blunt, John Archie Macdonald, Duncan J Macleod, Steve McCombe.
Front row: David Cameron, Duncan MacPherson, Kenny Mackay, Barbara Mackay, Linda Macdonald, Mary Maclennan.

NHT Steering Group:
Back row: Ronnie Morrison, Calum Mackay, Steve McCombe, Simon Fraser
Front row: Duncan J Macleod, Duncan MacPherson, David Cameron, Barbara Mackay, Kenny Mackay.

North Harris Trading Company:
Ronnie Morrison, David Cameron, Duncan MacPherson, Calum
Mackay, Duncan J Macleod, Alistair Macleod.

Loch Seaforth Steering Group:
Alan Woodward, Duncan MacPherson, David Moorhouse, Kenny
Mackay, Alistair Macleod, Simon Fraser.

The Sir E Scott School Senior Choir on a trip to the Pan-Celtic Festival in Ireland. The North Harris Trust provided financial support for the trip.

Murdo Morrison, one of the first directors of the North Harris Trust.

Donald J. Morrison, Director of North Harris Trust

Ian Scarr-Hall.

Marion Morrison & Calum Morrison (no relation) of Comhairle nan Eilean Siar counting the ballots, with Ian Leather, Deputy Returning Officer, looking on.

Announcing the formal result.

Crowd walking from the Scaladale centre to the Ardvourlie Woodland on the day the community took formal possession of the land.

L to R – David Cameron (Vice-Chair), Simon Fraser & Calum MacKay (Chair).

David Cameron speaking after Simon Fraser had passed a sample of North Harris soil to him (in blue pouch).

Joanna Morrison planting a tree to commemorate the community purchase.

Allan Wilson, deputy Environment Minister with Brian Wilson MP in the background.

People with spades etc – a group of John Muir Trust volunteer
workers undertake footpath repairs, with NHT director Kenny
Mackay in the foreground.

A helicopter lifting material to reconstruct the
Urgha – Reinigeadal path in January 2007.

to crofters and the wider community, in order for people to make a considered decision. (Feasibility Study, p. 26, 3.4.)

It has to be said that the majority of the meetings were not well-attended. Nonetheless, an impressive number of practical suggestions about potential job creation were made by those who did attend the public meetings, and those ideas were incorporated in the Feasibility Study. Disappointingly, many of the school pupils felt that, as they would all be leaving the island for further education and probably finding work on the mainland thereafter, the buy-out did not concern them. The Steering Group was considerably dismayed about what the apparent apathy and misunderstandings might imply for a ballot on the outcome of the Feasibility Study. The most worrying of these misunderstandings was about the availability of external funding. For instance, the report on both the meeting with the Grazings Clerks and with the school pupils revealed similar misconceptions, which must have been indicative of the misconceptions in the wider community. The report on the meeting with the Grazings Clerks said:

'The fundraising and/or borrowing required to be undertaken by the community in order to obtain the funds for purchase were a major concern (to those attending the meeting) and there was no clear understanding of the level of funds required. The general feeling was that the community would be unable to raise funds quickly enough and to take on borrowing would be a major consideration. If this reflects the general view, then few will realistically consider the advantages and disadvantages of community ownership without further information on funding potential, as it (community ownership) appears either to be (a) unlikely to be an achievable option or (b) one that would be financially burdened by debt from the outset.' (Feasibility Study, 3.3, p. 26.)

And again from the meeting with the school pupils:

'There was a general impression that the purchase of the estate by the community would involve large borrowing and, based on this understanding, they sensibly felt that the debt would be unserviceable. This perhaps indicates a commonly held belief that the community would need to borrow substantial sums of money to cover the full purchase price that would be both an impossible burden to repay and hamper other development through its demands on any funds.' (Feasibility Study, 3.4, p. 27.)

What had been forgotten, or perhaps was never fully understood by the community, was that at the public Meeting on 13th May, John Watt had answered the question about what assistance would be available to the community if they decided to opt for a buy-out by saying:

'The Land Fund can pay for up to 75% of the cost of land purchase, with the CLU contributing 75% of the difference. This leaves the community with a minimum of 6% to pay.'

These misconceptions alone, without taking into account natural caution and actual antipathy to a buy-out, made it only too clear that the Steering Group had serious obstacles to tackle in a very short timescale if there was to be any prospect of the community giving a positive response in a ballot on the conclusion of the Feasibility Study.

In addition to a thorough assessment of all aspects of the Estate in the process of formulating a potential business plan, Graeme Scott and his fellow consultants had to explore in depth the wishes and expectations of the Steering Group. In the course of these discussions, which were dominated as so often happened by the recurrent problem of Amhuinnsuidhe Castle, one significant question arose, and this question was to become of paramount importance: How would the community interact with a commercial partner running the Castle, and what conditions could reasonably be stipulated to such a partner?

Of course, a partner need not be considered only in relation to the Castle. The Steering Group knew that both the John Muir Trust and Chris Brasher had put money into Knoydart. As much of North Harris consisted of wild land, they could consider environmental groups such as the John Muir Trust or the Scottish Wildlife Trust as potential partners. One factor that was important to the Steering Group was to ensure that such partners were in the minority on any Board of Directors of a potential Trust. Graeme Scott emphasised to them that it was important that any conditions imposed on a partner should not be prohibitively restrictive and should, if necessary, allow any potential partner to make a profit so that his participation would be worthwhile. Accepting that a suitable partner in a buy-out might solve some of their problems, the Steering Group decided to ask Jonathan Bulmer to have his selling agents advise potential buyers that the community might be interested in partnership agreements.

While the pace of these policy and strategy meetings in mid-June might have seemed relatively relaxed, a number of urgent administrative tasks had to be instigated in order to meet the deadline of a September closing date. The valuation of the Estate had still to be commissioned, either by Highlands and Islands Enterprise or by the Steering Group. This information had then to be incorporated in the Feasibility Study. An in-depth study of the operations at the Castle by a hotel specialist was required. Simon Fraser's legal work for the Steering Group on the Memorandum and Articles for a potential Trust and his work for the consultancy team were to be rolled into the overall contract. Because a strict timetable for the duration and presentation of the Feasibility Study had already been decided, it became necessary for the CLU to fund an extra three days work by the Consultancy team to allow for a specialist in hotel management to visit Amhuinnsuidhe. This led to a revision of the timetable for submission of an interim report and then for submission of the final report from the Consultants. They decided that the interim report should be submitted and circulated to the members of the Steering Group by Tuesday 16 July, and a final report was to be ready a fortnight later. As this timetable would take them into August, they were all aware that it was going to be difficult to hold a ballot and meet a September deadline for a bid for the Estate, if that were to be the community decision. (Minutes of NHCSG Meeting, 18 June, 11pm and 26 June, 2002 5.30 pm.)

At the end of June, the long-promised visit to Knoydart took place. Kenny MacKay, Duncan MacLeod and Donald MacLennan were the Steering Group representatives on this visit. They reported that:

> *'The place was buzzing the night we stayed there. There were 120 guest beds filled that night for a population of only 70 residents. There were 3 separate companies covering the land and buildings, the forestry and the Hydro scheme. The first problem the Knoydart community faced was the sale of Inverie House. A local couple had offered £15,000, but the Trust sold it to the highest bidder for £40,000, a decision which split the community. However the money had gone towards the Hydro project which had benefited everyone in the community.'*

The North Harris Community Steering Group felt that the young people in Knoydart had a far greater interest in the project and that there was a greater community atmosphere in Knoydart than there was in North Harris. On the post-buy-out situation the visitors reported that:

> *'The current problems faced in Knoydart are a lack of accommodation, the sewage system, and the need for a new pier which would allow for a bigger boat to bring lorries over which could remove timber for sale. Although they had heard that there were some residents opposed to community ownership, none of the visitors actually met anyone who spoke against it.'* (NHCSG Minute 26 June 2002.)

By mid-July, the interim report from the Consultancy team was ready. The report was comprehensive. It included the valuation of the estate as well as a thorough examination of the options for developing the different sources of estate income. A wide range of opportunities had been identified by the consultancy team, both at the public consultations and, in particular, from their own assessment of the estate. At the meeting to discuss the report, Steering Group members felt that the potential sources of income were encouraging. Although few people were currently employed on the Estate full-time, there was the potential to increase the level of employment and income through environmental schemes and projects. For instance, it had been established that 80% of anglers returned more than once to Harris, and for that reason the possibilities for increasing the fishing were promising. However, predictably there were discouraging aspects to the Report, and most of these involved Amhuinnsuidhe Castle. The limitations of the castle were all too clear. The potential profit from the castle and associated operations was too small and too dependent on key individuals. Necessary upgrading of the house would be expensive. It seemed that capital expenditure might be needed to upgrade the fabric of the Castle before trading could begin. The income from the Castle only appeared to be generating a moderate surplus without fully maintaining the Castle. The question as to how much space a manager at the Castle would take up had not been taken into consideration when looking at the expansion of guest quarters.

In the light of all the unanswered and indeed unanswerable questions about the Castle, the Steering Group agreed that they would not want to go to the stage of a Final Report without a partnership scheme being developed as a clear option. The scenario envisaged was the possibility of a partner buying or leasing the Castle, the salmon fishing and the shooting rights, leaving the other resources in the hands of the local community. They also wanted the extent of potential job creation to be clearly defined and highlighted in the Final Report, to show the benefits of community ownership to those who currently saw little benefit in it. As a result of the consultations with the community, the Steering Group asked that in the Final Report the Consultancy team should highlight the role of a manager of a potential Trust, because many in the community feared day-to-day decision-making by committee. Everyone accepted that finding a partner willing to be part of a community buy-out was the key to further progress with the project.

It must have been difficult for members of the Steering Group to be constantly aware of how fragile the project was, to be preoccupied simultaneously with the complex details of the Feasibility Study, and yet to turn their attention to the necessary preparations for the constitution of a hypothetical Community Trust which would put in a bid for the Estate – if that was the eventual decision of the community in a ballot. The evening after the meeting on the Consultancy Team's interim report, Simon Fraser presented the Steering Group with a draft of the *Memorandum and Articles of Association*. Decisions had to be taken about eligibility for membership and voting rights in a Trust, the election of a fully representative Board of Directors, and when directors should retire. At all times people were aware of the need to avoid the perception that the village of Tarbert would dominate the Trust. The final decision was that the principle of geographic representation should be used for the Trust, with Tarbert having four directors, and then one each from Ardvourlie-Bowglass, Ardhasaig to the head of Loch Meavaig, Urgha to Glen Carragreich, Caolais Scalpaigh, and Hushinish/ Govig/ Amhuinnsuidhe, making a total of nine directors. (Minutes of NHCSG Meeting , 18 July 2002.)

Studying the report, even at its interim stages, was an exceptional learning experience for members of the Group. The report was of great use in focusing the minds of the Steering Group on the multi-faceted potential of the estate assets, on the drawbacks of aspiring to buy the whole estate and manage it single-handedly, and on the option of some kind of partnership arrangement. It would probably be fair to say that no single person on the Steering Group could have had at their finger-tips the extensive knowledge of the estate and its potential which this comprehensive study made available. July was drawing to an end. August held the prospect of the final Feasibility Report, with its recommendations one way or the other, the responsibility of putting these recommendations to the community, and the momentous decision to be taken on the way ahead.

Chapter 6
Towards the Ballot

The months of July and August are probably the busiest months for most people in the Western Isles. The vital tourist industry, on which so many incomes depend, is at its height with bed and breakfasts fully-booked and caravans and tents on every site. Calmac runs an almost non-stop ferry service to the islands; families come 'home' on holiday (a tradition which still endures, despite the lure of the Mediterranean sun); the regular fishing visitors and holiday-home people (who would not count themselves as tourists) arrive and, of course, for the islanders themselves, there are school holidays for those who want to get away to the mainland or further afield. These are also the months when the islands are at their most strikingly beautiful. North Harris does not have the conspicuous beauty of the white shell-sand beaches on the machair side of South Harris. Its beauty is more austere, with the blue-black grandeur of mountain and rocks, the subdued shades of moorland and a rare quality of light and shadow as cloud and sunlight alternate across the peaks. Visitors, be they curious reporters or well-disposed members of the general public, wonder why anyone might want to buy this almost lunar landscape. It is all too easy to misunderstand the motives underlying the aspirations of the North Harris community.

July and August also represent the 'silly season,' when less responsible members of the national press dredge up their more bizarre offerings of sensation and gossip. Summer 2002 was no exception to this pattern. Much was made in the press of the potential buy-out of the largest Highland estate, with its famous fishings and its fairy-tale castle. There was a strong suggestion that either politics or greed was the driving force in the buy-out. One of the wilder headlines declared, *'Celebrities line up to become island laird.'* (*Observer*, 7 July 2002.) Among the line-up of possible purchasers offered over the course of the summer were Madonna, Sting, Mohammed Al Fayed, Paul McCartney, Michael Jackson and Nick Faldo. Wherever it was coming from, such sensationalist nonsense seriously underestimated the sophistication of people in Harris. One local commentator responded by saying, 'First it was Madonna. Faldo visited here once and put a fiver in the Golf Club box, so now it must be him. Before that it was John Kerr and Sting. They were here once and it didn't rain, so they said they liked the place, apparently. It seems that no link, however tenuous, can be left without being milked to put us all off the idea and to convince us that we have no chance of achieving this.' (*Press & Journal,* 17th June 2002.) Throughout September, as the ballot drew nearer, such pressure increased, with condescending references to Compton Mackenzie and Ealing comedies from *Scotland on Sunday (SOS* 20 Sept. 2002). An equally disparaging piece in '*Écosse*' in the *Sunday Times* also trotted out the Ealing comedy line (15 Sept 2002). The *Daily Telegraph's* Scottish correspondent provided a more balanced, if still discouraging headline: 'Islanders "Lukewarm" on Bulmer Buy-out' (*Daily Telegraph,* Wed. Sept. 11, 2002).

Those who were closely involved with the Steering Group remember a frenetic summer with meetings almost every day, a constant sense of pressure, and a sense of nagging uncertainty as to whether it would all come together in the end. As Duncan MacPherson and Kenny Mackay had asked themselves on the evening of 29th April, what had they let themselves in for? By 20th August, the final report on the Feasibility Study was in the hands of the Steering Group with Simon Fraser in Tarbert, ready for a video-link to Inverness where John Watt (CLU) was waiting with two of the Consultancy Team, Graeme Scott and Steve Westbrook. Graeme Scott summarised the situation facing the Steering Group. The North Harris Estate had been placed on the open market in April 2002, inviting offers over £4.5 million. The Estate comprised some 55,000 acres, of which approximately 20,000 acres were subject to crofting tenure. On offer was Amhuinnsuidhe Castle with – in varying states of repair or disrepair – other estate buildings, and the land, with all its development potential. Part of the Estate's income came from salmon and sea trout fishings, brown trout loch fishing, coastal and sea fishing and the deer forest. The Castle had a good anchorage and slipway. A number of leases, principally relating to fish farming and wayleaves, also generated an annual income. The number of official designations of sites of special scientific and environmental interest reflected the outstanding natural heritage of the Estate.

The key considerations taken into account in the Feasibility Study had been:
(1) a realistic assessment of the likelihood of funding for the purchase of the Estate being available, within a relatively short timescale, from the Scottish Land Fund, the Community Land Unit and from other sources;
(2) the ongoing financial viability of the Estate while taking into account the risk of not achieving projected income;
(3) the retention of existing Estate employment and the scope to generate new employment opportunities;
(4) protecting the valuable fishing and sporting resources;
(5) generating income and local employment through woodland development and environmental management agreements;
(6) the need to maintain the value of the Estate through carrying out repairs and maintenance, as required, to the Castle and the sea wall;
(7) the value to the local community of having an Estate landlord sympathetic to sustainable economic and environmental development; and finally,
(8) providing the opportunity to develop facilities and activities that would broaden the tourism base of Harris and increase the impact from visitors.

The Consultancy Team had assessed the benefits and costs of three possible scenarios. These options were summarised as follows:

Option 1: the community purchasing all the estate assets;

Option 2: the community purchasing the land and certain other assets in conjunction with a partner who would purchase the castle and lease sporting and possibly fishing rights from the community;

Option 3: a 'crofting community group' purchasing only the croft land. (Feasibility Study, Introduction, p. 1, 1.3.)

As with the discussion of the interim Feasibility Study, each member of the Steering Group was given an opportunity to ask questions and to express their views on the final report. By the end of the meeting, a clear consensus had been reached.

Option 1 – that was for the community to buy all the assets of the Estate – was ruled out. The difficulties lay in raising the capital to buy the whole Estate. Additionally, the risks associated with maintaining the profitability of the whole estate, in particular the Castle, were too high. While some of those present were sorry to relinquish the thought of buying the Castle, they realised that the risks of doing so were too great to consider. (Minutes of NHCSG Meeting, 20 August 2002.)

Option 3 – that was purchase of the croft land alone – was ruled out because it was one which could be taken up at any time under Crofting law. Also, in confining themselves to buying only the croft land, they would risk losing the opportunity to buy additional land and sporting rights. (NHCSG Minutes 20 August 2002.)

The decision of the Steering Group was to go with Option 2. This option meant a joint purchase by the community, with a partner owning the Castle and certain other assets. The community would attempt to purchase only part of the Estate i.e. the land, the rental assets, and some of the buildings. The Castle and fishings would be excluded. This option was considered by the Consultants, the Steering Group and their advisors in the Community Land Unit to be the option which was 'the most realistic and financially beneficial to the community.' (NHCSG Estate Purchase Proposal, 09 Sept. 2002.) Above all, this option would avoid taking on the intractable problem of the Castle.

Of course, Option 2 was dependent both on finding a suitable partner, and above all, on the community approving that option in a ballot. During the course of the discussion about the need to go to the community with a clear plan of action and a definite partner, John Watt took the opportunity to announce that he had been approached by a land agent on behalf of a potential partner. In addition, the John Muir Trust had expressed an interest in playing a role in the buy-out, but preferred that the community should initiate any discussion about how this might be accomplished. The Steering Group agreed that they should speak to the John Muir Trust.

As a consequence of the unanimous decision by the Steering Group that they would go to the community with a recommendation that they should bid for only part of the estate, there were some urgent tasks to be set in motion. A decision was needed on how the information about the recommended option was to be made available to the community and the press. Preparations had to be made for a public meeting and a postal ballot. A date for a meeting with the John Muir Trust had to be agreed in order to explore co-operation between the two bodies before the ballot took place. Because of the imminence of the closing date for the bid for the Estate, the Steering Group had to meet urgently with Jonathan Bulmer, to inform him of their decision and to ask his selling agent for a two-week extension to the closing date. At that meeting with Jonathan Bulmer and his selling agent, it became clear that an extension to the closing date was unlikely to be granted. While the Bulmer Trustees would 'look at' a bid for only part of the estate, they would be more likely to accept a suitable bid for the whole of the estate from any interested party. (NHSG Minute 27 August 2002.)

By the end of August, pressure on the Steering Group was increasing by the day. At least there was some prospect of finding a potential partner in the shape of the person whose land agent had contacted John Watt. To explore this possibility, a meeting was arranged between representatives of the Steering Group,

John Watt and Sandra Holmes with a representative of the person who had expressed an interest in a partnership agreement with the community. The first meeting with this potential buyer's representative was reasonably promising. At a meeting some days later with the person in question it became clear that he would not be a suitable partner in a North Harris community . Disappointing although that encounter with a potential partner may have been, the visit from Nigel Hawkins, Director of the John Muir Trust, to a Steering Group meeting on 27 August was entirely positive.

Addressing the Steering Group, Nigel Hawkins described the purpose and activities of the John Muir Trust. He told them that it had been formed in 1983 in order to protect and conserve wild places, and to increase awareness and understanding of the value of such places. At the time it owned seven estates, including three on Skye and one in the northern part of Knoydart. JMT supported community buy-outs and worked in partnership with local communities. It believed that local people were the best guardians of the environment. The John Muir Trust itself was interested in the natural and cultural heritage, and the history and agriculture of an area. It had considerable experience of working with local communities. It could help with appeals to its own membership, and with advice on conservation and the recreational value of land. It could carry out research surveys and these could be used as a basis for crofter forestry schemes, among other things.

Although members of the Steering Group had some prior knowledge of the John Muir Trust, they were keen to discuss how it might operate as a potential partner in North Harris. The areas explored covered decision-making by JMT directors on a board, help with funds for purchase and for future development, policies on fish farming, public access, shooting, and other policy areas. Nigel Hawkins said that the community must first decide if it wanted other partners. He believed that the community should be in control (for example, he said that the external JMT directors had never voted against a local community) but he believed that there was scope for other bodies to help. JMT could possibly assist with funds towards purchase. While the Trust did want to keep places wild and beautiful, JMT recognised that there had to be a balance between conservation and development. It valued public access, and fish farming was seen as vital in the area. JMT supported green energy (e.g. their support for the Knoydart Hydro-Electric Scheme) but he felt that it was important to give a lot of thought to how such a scheme might fit in with the environment. (Minute of NHCSG Meeting, 27 August 2002.)

Over the next two weeks the collaboration between the Steering Group and the John Muir Trust developed positively, with the prospect of establishing a partnership becoming increasingly likely. This encouraging relationship did much to boost morale for people who were under tremendous pressure, with a bid for the estate due to be made within little more than a fortnight.

Four major steps were taken in early September to inform the community and seek their support. Realising that it was unlikely that many people would have the time or inclination to read through the whole of the 98-page Feasibility Study, the Steering Group prepared a two-page 'Executive Summary of the Estate Purchase Proposal' to be circulated with the ballot paper. The Summary described the details of the option recommended by the Steering Group and what they hoped to achieve by buying part of the estate. A special issue of the community newsletter, *Dé Tha Dol?* was published. It contained a series of endorsements by public figures and agencies in support of the recommendation from the Steering Group. Both these documents urged people to vote 'yes' in the forth-coming ballot. A public meeting was arranged at which the decision would be explained in detail and arrangements were made to hold a postal ballot with the votes to be counted on Tuesday 17th September 2002.

The gist of the Executive Summary was given in a letter sent to all voters in North Harris, urging them to vote 'yes' in the ballot:

FEASIBILITY STUDY OUTCOME

The Feasibility Study is now complete and is available in the office of Harris Development Ltd. in the Old Hostel, Tarbert for members of the North Harris community to read every day from 9 am to 5 pm until Friday 13 September. An Executive Summary is also available.
The proposal which the Steering Group are recommending is the purchase of part of the Estate i.e. the land, rental assets and some of the buildings. The Castle and fishings are excluded.

This is assessed by the Consultants as being the option which is 'the most realistic and financially beneficial to the community.'

The Steering Group believes that the community should follow this option in order to:

- Secure the 4 jobs at the Amhuinnsuidhe hatchery which could be threatened by a new owner wishing to terminate the lease.
- Secure grazing rights to non-croft land which could also be threatened by a new owner.
- Ensure that land and other resources could be made available in the future for local housing, business and community needs.
- Take advantage of future development opportunities e.g. renewable energy for the benefit of the whole community.

Income to pay for the running of the Estate would firstly come from fish farm and other rents and be supplemented by payments for environmental management agreements along the lines of the Lewis peatlands scheme.

The Estate would be profitable from Year 1.

HOW WILL COMMUNITY OWNERSHIP OPERATE?

If the community decides to bid for the part of the North Harris Estate as recommended, the bid will be made by a company called the North Harris Trust.

This company will have a membership open to anyone who is resident in the North Harris Estate area (including Tarbert), who lives elsewhere in Harris or Lewis but tenants a croft within the Estate, or who lives elsewhere but is actively working a croft within the Estate.

If the bid is successful the community will own the proposed assets through its ownership of the North Harris Trust.

The Trust would be managed by Directors who would be appointed by – and be answerable to - all of the members (each member having an equal vote). There would be 9 community directors elected on a geographical basis.

The day-to-day running of the Estate would be carried out by an administrator who would be answerable to the directors. The Scottish Land Fund would also provide funding for the first 3 years for a Development Officer who would develop new projects and income sources for the Estate.

The assets of the Trust – i.e. the estate – would be protected for all time by the Trust not engaging in any trading activity itself, but by carrying out any trading activity through subsidiary trading companies. If, for whatever reason, the Trust had to be wound up, the maximum that any member would have to pay would be strictly limited to only £1.

BALLOT

The purpose in sending this letter is so that you, as a member of the community, might have the opportunity to give your opinion on this proposal. We have therefore included a ballot paper for you to fill in and return. We would encourage you to vote so that a truly representative picture of local opinion might result from this process. The count will take place in the Community Centre in Tarbert on Tuesday 17th September at 11a.m. and you are welcome to attend.
On the basis of the findings of the feasibility study we encourage you to vote 'Yes'. (Extracted from NHCSG Community Letter, September 2002.)

At the end of April 2002, the majority of the members appointed to the North Harris Community Steering Group had approached the question of attempting a community buy-out with open minds; some were frankly sceptical about the proposal. By the end of August, after four months of serious discussion and research into the assets of the estate, they were all confident that the option of buying the land without the castle made good sense. With a mixture of relief and apprehension, they were able to hand over their recommendation to the community for the people of North Harris to decide on the way ahead.

Chapter 7
From the Ballot to the Bid

In marked contrast to the condescending attitude of much of the national press, the local press was very supportive of the North Harris community in their attempted buy-out. Under the heading, *'Over to you North Harris,'* the leader in the *West Highland Free Press* of 13 September 2002 read,

> *'Things look promising. The mood is positive. The groundwork has been thorough... Those who were opposed to a lesser or greater degree in the beginning are now committed supporters of a buy-out. This is the best news of all, and is hugely to the credit of those who are big enough to say that they have changed their minds... From the outset, we have said that this must be a decision for the community alone without outside pressure or interference. So on the eve of the ballot we make just one plea ... please do return that ballot paper... In the meantime, and whatever the outcome, we salute the North Harris Community Steering Group who have served their community so diligently and well.' (West Highland Free Press, 13 September, 2002.)*

While none of its admirers would claim that the *Free Press* had the gift of second sight, the words 'whatever the outcome' could not have been more percipient. When the recommendation from the Steering Group was announced to the community in early September, nobody could have anticipated the imminent roller coaster of apparent success followed by disappointment which was to sweep them along for the next six months. Looking back on it, the events of that autumn and winter might be compared to a succession of breakers crashing remorselessly to shore, battering the Steering Group and then the North Harris Trust as they sought a suitable partner and submitted one bid after another. Their difficulties were compounded by the fact that

71

decisions taken were almost always provisional, dependent on the outcome of events out with their control.

Despite the unsuccessful negotiations with a potential partner in late August, the Steering Group decided that, if the community vote was favourable, they would go ahead with a solo bid for the estate, excluding the castle and fishings. An application for funding had to be prepared and, again depending on the outcome of the ballot on 17th September, submitted in time to meet the closing date of 19 September. Tight though the timetable was, the application for funding was held in abeyance until 18th September, when the result of the ballot was known to be positive.

Monday 9th September was chosen as the date for the public meeting, just over a week before the votes were due to be counted in Tarbert. There had been some anxiety about the advisability of holding a public meeting at the beginning of the week which would include all the traditional church services in preparation for the weekend Communions. It is difficult for strangers to island culture to understand that the weeks of the spring and autumn Communions have a deep religious significance for those who are church members, when worldly affairs take second place to the spiritual. On a purely practical level, for the women in the community it is also a very busy week, as visitors from other congregations have to be housed and fed with typical island hospitality, when they come to attend church services from the Thursday till the following Monday. It used to be, and to a lesser extent still is, a week of cleaning the house from top to bottom, moving the family into make-shift beds to make rooms available for visitors, filling all the tins with home-made baking, cooking in advance as much as can be stored, and delivering gifts of food to the manse to feed the most important visitors of all: the assisting ministers. The fear of the Steering Group was that a meeting about something as apparently remote and secular as the purchase of the estate might not be seen as a top priority for everyone.

Nonetheless, an audience of seventy-five people was present in the Community Centre in Tarbert on the night of the public meeting. Both politicians and members of the press were excluded, as the meeting was deemed to be for the local people only. David

Cameron, a member of the Steering Group, had been chosen to speak in support of the recommendation to purchase only the land and its associated assets without the castle and fishings. He said:

> 'My part in the meeting tonight is very straightforward. It is to speak on behalf of the Steering Group to outline briefly why we have chosen the recommendation on which the community is being balloted.
>
> The recommendation is to bid for the land of North Harris Estate with shooting rights, other rights, rental assets, the Stable Block, the buildings at the jetty and the boat shed and slip. Putting it another way, this excludes the Castle, its salmon fishing rights, and the houses associated with the fishing at Tolmachan and Kinlochresort.
>
> After listening to your comments when this whole process started, it was agreed by all the members of the Steering Group that, whether a bid was for all or part of the Estate, the bid had to fulfil four certain conditions.
>
> One, we had to be confident that the Estate could be managed, operated and developed effectively, safeguarding existing jobs, the rights of the people and the natural heritage.
>
> Two, the financial risk to the community should be low.
>
> Three, the community should be able to run the part of the Estate in our bid, at a profit.
>
> Four, that the difference between the buying price and the money available from funding bodies, i.e. the money which we would have to raise as a

community, should not be a burden and restrict development.

Looking at each of these in turn: -

The first point: - we had to be confident that the Estate could be managed, operated and developed effectively, safeguarding existing jobs, the rights of the people and the natural heritage. This might be in conjunction with partners with whom the community feels comfortable. We believe that we have come up with a structure which meets the above in full, and which Duncan MacPherson will explain later.

The second point: - the financial risk to the community should be at a low level. This was one of the main reasons that we cannot recommend a bid for the Castle with associated salmon fishing. However, without these, the main risks are removed.

The third point: - the community should be able to run the part of the Estate in our bid, at a profit. In fact, the report shows that the recommended option can start producing a profit even in year one and with development, this profit is forecast to rise in subsequent years.

And finally, and perhaps most importantly, the fourth point: - the difference between the buying price and the money available from funding bodies (i.e. the money which we would have to raise as a community) should not be a burden and restrict development.

We cannot release too much financial information, for the obvious reason that we are in a competitive bidding situation and there are many people out there who would be delighted to know the level of our bid. However, with anticipated maximum support from the funding bodies, with financial contributions from such people as the John Muir Trust, and most importantly with a positive result in the ballot, we have total confidence in saying that if the bid went in tomorrow, the amount we would still have to find would be in the region of £50,000.

We also believe that there are many other sources of funding both within and without Harris, and the amount required is very achievable.

We also believe and recommend that a fund is set-up for development purposes and it too should have a target of £50,000.

Whatever way you look at this, this must represent exceptional value, not only to us but to generations down the line. Thank you.'

(North Harris Community Steering Group's Recommendation Presentation at Public Meeting, 09 September 2002.)

If, at the public meeting on 13 May, John Murdo Morrison had represented the doubts and fears of many people about a potential community buy-out, he may also have represented the transformation of public opinion four months later. As soon as David Cameron had finished speaking, John Murdo Morrison stood up to say that he was now persuaded of the merits of the case for a buy-out. The reaction of the audience has been compared to the switching-on of a light. Apart from a palpable sense of relief among the members of the Steering Group, there was the realisation that if one major sceptic had been persuaded by the strength of the case put forward, there was a fair chance that many others would share his conviction.

Whether it was the positive mood of that meeting, the contents of the letter accompanying the ballot form, the endorsements by public agencies such as Comhairle nan Eilean Siar, Highlands and Islands Enterprise and individual members of the Steering Group published in *Dé Tha Dol?* or simply favourable word of mouth between friends and neighbours that had influenced public opinion, it was becoming clear on the grapevine well before the count that the vote had swung in favour of bidding for the estate.

The count took place in the Village Hall Tarbert on Tuesday 17th September in the presence of the Steering Group and any members of the community who wanted to be there. Despite the earlier intimations of success, the process of opening the envelopes, extracting the ballot forms and flattening them out, allocating them to separate piles and seeing the *'yes'* pile growing higher and higher was excruciatingly tense for the watchers. At last the result of the ballot was announced:

> *'I, Ian Leather, Depute Returning Officer for the Community Ballot held in North Harris regarding the proposal to purchase the North Harris Estate, declare that the total number of ballot papers returned was 401 and that votes were cast as follows:*
>
> *Yes: 302 votes*
> *No: 99 votes*
> *There were NIL spoiled papers.*
>
> *I further declare that the community has voted in favour of the proposal.*
>
> *Ian Leather, Depute Returning Officer, 17 September 2002.'*

That result reflected a 74% return of ballot papers (401 votes from an electorate of 539) with 75% (302) in favour of the proposal and 25% (99) against it.

Relief, mixed with an element of disbelief; delight, mixed with cautious excitement, in the knowledge that this was but the first hurdle on the way to a successful bid – all these emotions were apparent among those who had worked so hard to reach this moment. Kenny MacKay, Chairman of the North Harris Community Steering Group, said:

> '*It's been an historic week in every way. The voting was really good, with a good turnout - especially bearing in mind that the papers were saying at the weekend that we had no chance of making the deadline.*'

The editorial in *The West Highland Free Press* that week gave a balanced analysis of the local response:

> '*The ballot result in North Harris represents a triumph of good sense and hope for the future over the sense of caution which is inherent in island communities. Above all perhaps, it is a tribute to the leadership which has been shown within the community itself.*
>
> *As we noted last week, the work of the North Harris Community Steering Group has been exceptional. They have taken people with them and have made no grandiose assumptions about what the community might go along with. Hearts and minds have been won because they have been argued for on a rational and reasonable basis, backed up with hard evidence.*
>
> *North Harris is not a community in extremis. Although the hand of the estate has always been strongly felt, it is not a place which is reeling under the malign influence of vicarious proprietors as has been the case in some other buy-out areas. North Harris is already a strong community and an excellent place to live and work.*
>
> *This makes the outcome of the ballot all the more*

significant. It is a thoughtful vote about how the place can help itself in future and the role that land can play in that process. It is less a vote against something, than one in favour of a future in which people can play a greater part in shaping their own destiny.

Of course, the community buy-out is not yet home and dry. The outcome still depends on the current owner. However, as someone who is recognised to have a genuine concern for the well-being of North Harris, it seems unlikely that he would have allowed this well-publicised process to advance so far, only to frustrate it at the last moment. Next week we shall know for sure.

Nobody in Harris, however they voted in this week's ballot, will dispute the clear-cut validity of the outcome. A three-to-one majority on a turnout of over three-quarters is by any standards, outside those of North Korea, pretty impressive. And, in the wider land reform debate, that is a statement of some significance.'

(WHFP 20 Sept. 2002.)

As if all the fates were looking benignly on Harris that week, there was a run of good news. Sandra Holmes had informed the Steering Group that the Scottish Land Fund had unanimously approved a grant of £1,665,750 and that there would be a Highlands and Islands Community Land Fund grant of £416,438. Nigel Hawkins had written to offer funding of £100,000 from the John Muir Trust for the purchase and management of the estate. The selling agents had confirmed that they had received the bid of £2.11m with an entry date of 31 January 2003 and would be meeting within a week to give it their consideration. The most encouraging news of all was that a very acceptable potential partner had contacted the selling agents and John Watt at the Community Land Unit, to express an interest in those parts of the estate that the community did not want. The name Ian

Scarr-Hall was already well-known in Harris, both because of his long association with the island and because of his generous support for voluntary and charitable work in Harris. A more welcome initiative than the appearance of Ian Scarr-Hall as a potential partner at this stage in the project would be hard to imagine.

Ian Scarr-Hall is one of a long line of strangers to the islands who over the years have come to belong, in so far as anyone not born and bred there can belong. Their links with the islands are forged by respect and affection for the people and the place. Their sentiments come to be reciprocated as these strangers prove their long-term loyalty. Far removed from the formal language of the press release issued is Ian Scarr-Hall's own account of his coming to Harris as a young boy, staying in a cottage at Amhuinnsuidhe, and having the temerity to ask a keeper for permission to fish – and his annual return to a family home at Meavaig over the ensuing forty years. Equally far-removed from the language of the press release is the way in which those who know of his generosity to Harris welcomed his involvement in the Trust. As it turned out, his intervention in the buy-out was to make the difference between eventual success and very possible failure for the North Harris Trust.

With a degree of sympathetic insight not always found in visitors, Ian Scarr-Hall speaks of his experience of Harris:

> '... throughout my forty years of visiting, I have experienced wonderful, open Hebridean welcomes. It seems to me that the struggles of the people of the crofting community and those of their ancestors represent values and traditions which should be preserved for future generations. From the times of the Clearances and through the war years, the community has given greatly under conditions of extreme hardship. It was impossible to conceive that they could ever become landowners with responsibility for their own and their families' destiny. I see it as a great privilege to be a participant in this historic achievement.'

A far cry indeed from presenting oneself at the door of the castle asking for permission to fish! But even with such a welcome partner, the way ahead was not without moments when failure seemed almost inevitable.

With the outcome of the ballot and the submission of a bid for the estate, the work of the North Harris Community Steering Group was done. Their last meeting was held on Friday 20th September 2002, when the Steering Group was formally dissolved. That same evening the North Harris Trust came into being, with an interim set of office-bearers who would continue until such time as elected directors were appointed to represent all nine geographical areas of North Harris. Those interim office-bearers were: Chairman, David Cameron; Vice-Chairman, Calum Mackay; Treasurer, Ronnie Morrison, and Company Secretary, Duncan MacPherson. Other members of the defunct Steering Group were invited to attend meetings until an election to appoint directors from geographical areas was held. Councillor Morag Munro and retiring Chairman Kenny MacKay were included for the time being, although their addresses were out with the boundaries of North Harris. (Minute of Meeting of NHT 20 Sept 2002.)

A number of administrative items were transacted at that first meeting of the North Harris Trust, including plans for a fund-raising appeal as soon as the result of the bid was known. The John Muir Trust was officially invited to become a member of the Trust, and asked to appoint one director plus an alternate director, neither of whom would be directly involved in the negotiations for the buy-out. (The JMT subsequently appointed Nigel Hawkins and Will Boyd-Wallis as their directors on the Trust.)

However, the first and most important item on the agenda on 20th September was the formal and unanimous adoption of the Bye-Laws of the Company (Minute of NHT Meeting 20 September 2002, p. 2) which had been prepared by Simon Fraser in anticipation of the formation of a North Harris Trust, which would take over from the Steering Group when it came to the point of submitting a bid. The bye-laws, which had been formulated by members of the Steering Group in consultation with Simon Fraser, were very specific in defining who was entitled to become a member of the Trust and the areas from which Directors of the Trust were to be appointed: four from Tarbert and five from out with Tarbert. Of the latter five, two directors should be from east of Tarbert, two from west of Tarbert and one from over the Clisham. In order to ensure that the Community Directors would never be outnumbered by co-opted Directors, there would be a maximum of sixteen directors, and co-opted directors would be always be the exception to the rule rather than the norm. The matter arose at this point because of the need to observe those bye-laws in making arrangements for the first election of Directors and the conditions governing applications for membership of the Trust.

While the North Harris Community Steering Group appointed in May had a vital function in exploring the feasibility of making a bid for all or part of the estate, it had no legal status – or, to use the correct legal terminology, no legal persona that entitled it to enter into a contract or to place a bid for the estate with the funding, granted under strict conditions, of the Scottish Land Fund, Highlands and Islands Community Land Unit and other funding bodies. To acquire that legal persona or, in layman's terms, to become 'a separate legal entity,' it was necessary to register the North Harris Trust as a company under the Companies Act with the Registrar of Companies.

The document which creates any such company is called the *Memorandum and Articles of Association*. The *Memorandum* part of this document lays down the objects and purposes for which the company is created, and these are usually as wide and all-encompassing as possible. The *Articles of Association* stipulate the rules by which the objects and purposes of the company may lawfully be achieved. In this case, the company was to be 'a company limited by guarantee and not having a share capital.' The company was incorporated on 23rd August 2002, with its Registered Office being at The Old Hostel, Tarbert, Isle of Harris.

The *Memorandum* of the North Harris Trust states that the objects for which the company is registered are:

'1. to take all appropriate measures to conserve the natural heritage ... of North Harris for the benefit of the community and the public at large and to promote open public access thereto insofar as this is not detrimental to such conservation;

2. to promote trade and industry for the benefit of the general public;

3. to relieve poverty and provide help for the aged, handicapped and infirm and to advance education and other charitable purposes beneficial to the community;

4. to provide, or promote the provision of, housing for people in necessitous circumstances and also specially designed or adapted housing as may be required for the elderly, handicapped or disabled;

5. to develop, or promote the development of, infrastructure for the benefit of the general public, to improve communications throughout North Harris including piers, harbours, roads and bridges, provided always that any development of such infrastructure does not relieve the Local Authority of its statutory obligations.'

The document continues at considerable length, describing the ways in which these purposes may be achieved. *The Memorandum and Articles* of the North Harris Trust provide a blueprint for the future work of the North Harris Trust. In framing them, their legal adviser Simon Fraser was able to draw on his long experience in guiding communities engaged in earlier buy-outs, while still reflecting the individual aspirations of the North Harris Community Steering Group. Were it to become necessary for any reason to amend the rules governing membership of the North Harris Trust or the numbers of Directors (as was to happen, for example, in 2006 when the Seaforth Estate was reunited with

North Harris) it would be simpler for the Directors to change the bye-laws to admit an enlarged membership of the Trust than to call a full General Meeting to amend the *Memorandum and Articles*.

The high hopes of late September for a speedy decision on the purchase of the estate evaporated as the negotiations dragged on into October, into November and even to a second closing date in December. Despite saying in the first instance that they would consider a bid for only part of the estate, the selling agents were, quite naturally, unwilling to accept the original bid from the North Harris Trust for only part of the estate, because they preferred if at all possible to sell the estate as a whole. While Ian Scarr-Hall and the Trust were working very amicably towards making their own bids, the knowledge that the selling agents were still open for offers was a real source of anxiety. Other potential purchasers appeared and disappeared during these long, wearisome weeks. Another source of anxiety for the North Harris Trust was the knowledge that there was an imminent deadline on the award from the New Opportunities Fund. By November it looked increasingly unlikely that they could meet the deadline. Again, as had been the case before the community ballot, the Trust had also to look ahead and make provisional arrangements for the appointment of a Project Officer and an Administrator, on the assumption that they would eventually succeed in buying the estate. The resolution that had carried the community towards a successful ballot was surely put to the test by this unforeseen delay.

Chapter 8
The Bids

Although the bid submitted in September by the newly-created North Harris Trust to buy just part of the North Harris Estate was not accepted by the Bulmer family, the possibility of being able to formulate a new bid, with Ian Scarr-Hall as their partner in a joint buy-out of the whole estate, offered the Trust a new and more promising prospect. The outline of a potential joint bid had been laid out in the *Executive Summary* made available to the community by the Steering Group at the time of the ballot.

> 'The proposal which the Steering Group are recommending is the purchase of part of the Estate i.e. the land, rental assets and some of the buildings. The Castle and fishings are excluded.'
> (Executive Summary of Feasibility Study.)

and that, ideally, a partner would bid for the Castle and fishings.

> 'Provided that a partner can be found who would run and develop the Castle and tourism aspects of the Estate in ways that would benefit the community, the consultants recommend Option 2 as the most realistic and financially beneficial to the community. Ideally, a partnership along the lines of Option 2 (b) would be established, but this would be subject to negotiation with any potential partner.'
> (Executive Summary of Feasibility Study.)

Ian Scarr-Hall's expression of interest in buying those parts of the Estate which the community did not want to buy had come just too late for any bid from him to be included in the bid formulated by the North Harris Trust to meet the closing date of 19 September. When that first bid for only part of the estate fell by the wayside, it became imperative for the North Harris Trust to formulate a joint bid with a partner for the whole estate, in the hope that a second bid would stand a better chance of success. The urgency of this task was underlined by the fact that the selling agents had let it be known that they were still open for offers. The weeks of October and early November thus involved both parties, the North Harris Trust and Ian Scarr Hall, in working out the fine points of a new bid.

An example of the very complex details which had to be negotiated between the North Harris Trust and Ian Scarr-Hall was recorded in the Minutes of 21 October 2002:

> - 'A 5m strip of land either side of the salmon rivers and the solum of the lochs and main river stems would belong to Ian Hall, except for the Govig system that would remain with the community and Loch na Cleabhaig where the community would hold brown trout fishing rights and there would be no strip around the loch. The Trust will manage the 5m strips and will receive any payments from Scottish Natural Heritage related to that management.
> - Ian (Scarr) Hall to own Loch Leosaid, but the Trust would have water extraction rights and rights to lay pipes to sea for the removal of hatchery waste water.
> - In addition to the stable block and cottages, Ian (Scarr) Hall will also now take the derelict cottage at the end of the jetty. The Trust will own the block of cottages with the deer larder.'
> (Minutes of NHT Meeting, 21 October 2002.)

An interesting aspect of these complex negotiations was that Simon Fraser, who had guided the Trust through all the desk-bound legalities of the buy-out with such sterling dedication, undertook the challenge of walking the boundaries of the land with Ian Scarr-Hall's representatives. For those unfamiliar with the island, it is worth remembering that North Harris is what the John Muir Trust describes as 'wild land.' In summer, for the young and fit, walking these bounds would be a pleasant day's exercise. In late October, for the not-so-young and not-so-fit, with the probability of heavy mist, or worse – of howling winds and driving rain, walking these rough bounds would be a somewhat daunting challenge! It has to be said, and cannot be over-emphasised, that Simon Fraser's expertise and perseverance in negotiating the arrangements between the Trust and Ian Scarr-Hall were very important to the successful outcome of the bid. In fact, his whole contribution to the buy-out of the North Harris estate has earned Simon Fraser the admiration and gratitude of all who worked with him on that project.

Ian Scarr-Hall was undoubtedly most welcome to the North Harris Trust as a potential partner, but they also had a responsibility to speak to other interested parties, lest the partnership being discussed with Ian Scarr-Hall should fall through for any reason. While discussions between the Trust, Ian Scarr-Hall and the Bulmer family were taking place, other potential bidders were also expressing an interest in a variety of possible deals. One of the proposed deals presented by an interested party suggested that the community might get the eastern part of the estate, and the western part would be leased back to the Bulmers. There seemed to be a measure of ambivalence about the Bulmer family's attitude to relinquishing all interest in the estate. For instance there was, at one point, a suggestion that the family might want to retain the salmon netting rights in Loch Resort. There was also another suggestion that an agreement could be reached which would allow Sebastian Bulmer further input into the estate in the future. The neighbouring Ath Linne Estate was also interested in protecting its fishing rights on the eastern side of the island.

Yet another potential buyer made contact on behalf of a family trust, with a view to buying all but the croft land, in which he had no interest. Although it was explained to him at a meeting with representatives of the Steering Group that the community wished to own much more than the croft land, he appeared to be the most likely threat to a successful purchase by a North Harris Trust/Scarr-Hall partnership. (Minutes of NHT Meeting, 11 Nov. 2002.)

Towards the end of October, all the weeks of discussion and planning by the North Harris Trust with their preferred partners, Ian Scarr-Hall and the John Muir Trust, had come to fruition. Rather than have the news of the proposed partnership leak out in a disjointed fashion, the North Harris Trust, Ian Scarr-Hall and the John Muir Trust co-ordinated their announcements to the press and the community on Wednesday 23rd October 2002, thus catching the lunchtime and evening news programmes on radio and television and meeting the deadlines for the local papers. The North Harris Trust press release said:

> *'After thorough discussion with potential partners in recent weeks, The North Harris Trust are very happy to advise that we have now agreed to cooperate with Mr Ian Scarr-Hall with a view to presenting an offer for the North Harris Estate in its entirety. We feel confident that we have found a partner who shares the same aims and objectives as ourselves.*
>
> *Ian Scarr-Hall has had connections with Harris for many years, is familiar with the Estate and is known by local people. He has contributed personally to several Harris causes, particularly in the voluntary sector, and we are now looking forward to working with him in a business capacity.'*
> (Press Release from North Harris Trust, 23 Oct. 2002.)

With a courteous tribute to Jonathan Bulmer, Ian Scarr-Hall took the opportunity of his own press announcement to give a brief overview of the work of his company, something which was not well-known to the majority of people in Harris. He said:

> *'I fully support the endeavours of the Community Trust in their negotiations to purchase the North Harris Estate. The objectives of my company, George S Hall, aim to continue the present activities so ably developed by the present owner and, where*

possible, to extend these to provide conference and training facilities. The George S Hall company is actively involved in promoting environmental management for sustainability and bio-diversity in the UK, Europe and the USA. The location of the Estate lends itself ideally for the promotion of programmes devoted to the sustainability of our natural resources.'
(ISH Press Release 23 Oct. 02, in NHT files.)

The concepts of 'environmental management for sustainability and bio-diversity' made an appropriate combination with the aims of the John Muir Trust, the third partner in the agreement.

'The John Muir Trust is delighted that agreement is being sought by the North Harris Trust and Mr Ian Scarr-Hall to formulate a bid to buy the North Harris Estate in its entirety. Going into partnership with a sympathetic private owner is a bold and creative move and sets a new way forward for communities wishing to buy large estates where they do not wish to take on all the assets themselves. If the bid is successful, it will mean Mr Hall will own Amhuinnsuidhe Castle and the fishings, while the North Harris Trust will own and manage the land of the 55,000 acre estate. We are impressed by Mr Hall and his plans for the area which will secure and create jobs while recognising the outstanding quality of the environment of North Harris. If the bid is successful - and we are all hoping it will be – it will be an historic moment for North Harris and its people.'
(JMT press release, 23 Oct. 2002 in NHT files.)

The news that a realistic partnership capable of submitting a joint bid for the North Harris Estate had been created was very much in line with the Highlands and Islands (HIE) network objectives. It contributed to all three strategic priorities of their *Strengthening Communities* programme. These were: to promote investment in community assets and services; to develop community strengths, leadership and confidence, and to enhance the quality of the environment and culture. Because the first start-up grant had been exhausted, the Steering Group was awarded a second start-up grant of £2000 at this point, to cover ongoing administration costs, professional fees for business planning and accountancy, subsistence expenses for Directors attending meetings in Edinburgh and Inverness, support for the community's fund-raising campaign, and newsletters to update the community on the progress of the bid.

The climate in which the North Harris Trust was operating was very different to the comparatively relaxed atmosphere of the Steering Group. An application for start-up funding was the first necessity, and this was followed by an application to the Scottish Land Fund and the Community Land Unit for revenue assistance for the proposed posts of Development Officer and Administrator, should a bid be successful. Each offer of funding carried with it strict conditions as to accountability by the Trust in the form of receipts, work plans, targets and reviews. The greatest and most urgent responsibility for both the Trust and Ian Scarr-Hall was in finalising a bid to buy the Estate.

The separate, but complementary, bids by the North Harris Trust in conjunction with Ian Scarr-Hall for the North Harris Estate were unprecedented in the history of community buy-outs. Because there was no precedent for the type of buy-out envisaged, there was no tried and tested model to draw on. In earlier buy-outs such as that in Knoydart, the 'big house' (in that case, Inverie House) was part of the initial bid, and the house was then sold on to finance further development. In North Harris, the 'big house' i.e. Amhuinnsuidhe Castle was to be retained as an integral part of the over-all buy-out. It was clearly essential that the bids by each of the potential partners reflected the value of the various assets to be purchased. Contrary to the impression given by some of the more sensationalist newspapers, the funding available for a community is neither plucked out of thin air, nor yet out of the imagination of optimistic selling agents. It is based on an independent valuation of the assets to be acquired, in the case of the North Harris Estate, on a valuation by Bowlts, a firm of specialist rural chartered surveyors with particular experience in valuing rural properties throughout the north of Scotland. The level of grant available to the North Harris Trust for the purchase of the land would depend on the valuation by Bowlts.

The sale of Amhuinnsuidhe Castle and part of its contents to Ian Scarr-Hall was inordinately complex and involved weeks of negotiations – not only over the Castle, the land associated with it, and the fishings, but also over the items within the Castle which were to be bought by Ian Scarr-Hall. Anybody who has inherited bequests in a small domestic situation, e.g. 'Granny's clock, the blue vase and twelve silver teaspoons,' will know the frustrations of wandering through a house and still not being sure that they have correctly identified their bequests. Multiply that situation by at least tenfold and it is not difficult to imagine that, in addition to the Castle and its associated buildings, the task of including some of the contents of the Castle in his bid was a nightmare for Ian Scarr-Hall and his representatives. Pieces of furniture or pictures which had been valued and described as being in a particular room at the time of valuation did not necessarily remain in their original locations, and identifying them was far from easy. Niall Graham-Campbell, a Property Consultant with CKD Finlayson-Hughes (as it then was), had the task of acting on behalf of Ian Scarr-Hall in his negotiations. By 29th November 2002, it was possible for both the North Harris Trust and Ian Scarr-Hall to submit their separate bids.

With the support of the New Opportunities Fund, Highlands and Islands Enterprise, John Muir Trust, Scottish Natural Heritage, Comhairle nan Eilean Siar and together with local fund raising, the community was eventually able to offer £2.2 million for the land assets of the 55,000 acre estate. Nonetheless, although the bids had been submitted, there was a period of some weeks when the outcome was still uncertain. The immediate source of concern lay in the fact that the Trust knew that in all probability they were not the only bidders interested in the Estate. There were possibly as many as three other separate bids going in for the North Harris Estate from some of the people who had expressed an interest of one sort or another in purchasing part of the estate or entering some sort of partnership with the Trust. (Minute of NHT Meeting 2nd Dec 2002.) With such uncertainty over the outcome of the joint bid with Ian Scarr-Hall, it was with great relief that the Directors of the North Harris Trust received, on Thursday 12th December 2002, a copy of a letter from Brodies, the solicitors for the North Harris Estate, informing them that the Trust with Ian Scarr-Hall was the preferred bidder. (Minute of the NHT Meeting, Thursday 12th December 2002.)

The months between April and December 2002 had been fraught with excitement, with tension, with disappointments and then with renewed hope for all those involved in assessing and putting into effect plans for a community buy-out of the North Harris Estate. In April, nobody would have anticipated that by December so much progress would have been made. With the news that they were the preferred bidders, it seemed that the Trust could look forward to a new year in which they could plan to celebrate their historic achievement.

Chapter 9
Celebrations

The formal statement in the Minutes, '*Everyone present was happy with the news,*' does not convey the conflicting emotions felt by those present at that meeting on 12 December 2002 when they learned that the North Harris Trust were the preferred bidders. (Minute of NHT Meeting of 12th December 2002.) The minds of some of the Directors turned to all that had to be done, how quickly the formalities could be completed, how and when they could take entry to the estate, how and when they could safely announce the good news to the people of North Harris. Despite the surge of excitement, there was still in the minds of at least some of the committee an elemental sense of caution. They shared the ancient belief that rejoicing too soon was unwise, and that 'tempting Providence' was an invitation to disappointment. These reservations gave rise to an instinctive reluctance to plan too far ahead, to rejoice too soon. The letter from Brodies, the solicitors for North Harris Estate, made a number of points in relation to concluding missives which the Directors discussed, but perhaps they did not fully appreciate at the time the extent to which these details would slow down the process of taking over the estate. Wisely, as it transpired, they decided that an entry date at the end of February rather than the end of January should be negotiated. Even that date was somewhat optimistic. This inevitable delay had important implications for the funding approved by the Scottish Land Fund, which expired on 20 December 2002. An application to extend the period had been made in early December and granted until 20 March 2003, the same date as the expiry of the funding from Highlands and Islands Community Land Unit. (SCL/140/1/02 correspondence between SLF, NOP and NHT December 2002.)

Little significant progress was possible because of Christmas and New Year, but by early January Simon Fraser was able to report to the Directors that he had had a successful visit to Brodies in Edinburgh. Separate offers from the Trust and Ian Scarr-Hall were being re-drafted, and Brodies were confident that, once the detailed terms had been agreed, these offers would be accepted by the Bulmer family. However, an indication by Brodies of likely acceptance of the offers would by no means imply a speedy conclusion to the purchase of the estate. A thorough examination of the title deeds and leasing agreements, the compilation of maps of estate boundaries, the proportional allocation of rental income, the preparation of an agreed inventory of moveables in Amhuinnsuidhe Castle and many other legalities unfamiliar to the layman's mind had to be completed before finalising the buy-out. Yet again, Simon Fraser did a power of work in finalising what was a very complex conveyancing process. In fact, it was early March before final signatures were achieved.

However, with the prospect of the offer being accepted in the relatively near future, a number of urgent tasks had to be set in motion. The first priority was to arrange for the election of new Directors of the Trust to take over from the interim Directors who had been appointed when the Trust had been formed, in order to submit the bid. Another urgent task was to finalise the list of responsibilities for the Development Officer and the Administrator, who were to be appointed once the buy-out had been completed. It was stressed that the Administrator's post would be a stand-alone post and not an assistant to the Development Officer. Duncan MacPherson had prepared an application for financial assistance for these posts, and it was hoped that funding would be approved at the February meeting of the Scottish Land Fund. The Community Land Unit also contributed to the revenue funding package. Funding was approved in early March by SLF and HIE, to be awarded over three years. The announcement of this award was embargoed until the celebration of the buy-out on 21 March, 2003.

Sandra Holmes, who had guided and assisted both the North Harris Community Steering Group and the North Harris Trust over the significant months of 2002, was present at the meeting of 30 January 2003 to introduce Donnie Mackay, one of two CLU aftercare officers. He would take over from Sandra as the main point of contact once any purchase had gone through. Donnie Mackay explained that he would be there to provide continuing support to the Trust in developing its work in future years. The Directors were also told that further financial support could be applied for by them from the Scottish Land Fund for development projects, and that Trust members would be invited to future networking events at which ideas and experiences could be shared between community groups. (Minute of NHT Meeting, 30 January 2003.)

While the preparations for the buy-out were being processed, important consultations had also been taking place with Scottish Natural Heritage (SNH). Jonathan Bulmer and David Maclennan (Area Manager for SNH in the Western Isles) had discussed ideas for environmental management of sheep and deer on the North Harris Estate for some time before the estate had gone on the market. Over the preceding two years, SNH had been engaged in surveying and mapping vegetation communities across the estate and assessing the condition of the land. North Harris Trust submitted an application for funding to SNH on 3 December 2002. In February 2003 this application was rewarded with a grant offer of £40,000 in respect of the proposals for North Harris Estate Land purchase. The claim was to be submitted by 1 March 2003, and would be payable when missives for the sale of the estate had been exchanged. Some of the more important conditions attached by SNH to the award included the North Harris Trust '*upholding the exercise of access rights in accordance with the Scottish Outdoor Access Code, the preparation of a management plan within two years of entry; this plan would be subject to regular review; and access to the land would be available for members of SNH staff for the purposes of inspection, research, experimentation or scientific operation.*'

March 2003 reverted to the pattern of activity experienced in summer 2002, with committee meetings at least once a week. Much clearing of the decks had to be done in anticipation of finalising the buy-out. A major step forward took place on 4th March, when Simon Fraser attended a meeting of the Trust to say that he wished to send the purchase money for the buy-out to Brodies on Thursday 13th March. He also informed them that David Cameron, as Chair, would have to go to Edinburgh on Friday 14th March for the payment of the purchase price and to sign the missives. The Directors agreed unanimously to go ahead with these transactions.

When arranging for the election of new Directors, the committee had decided that nominations for Directors should be made by Wednesday 12th March, with ballot forms to go out by 14th March and returned by 19th March – a tight schedule by any standards. However, the intensity of interest was such that there was no need for elections, as a full complement of Directors was nominated (Minute of NHT Meeting 13th March 2003) and subsequently confirmed at the Inaugural General Meeting held on the evening of 19th March.

The Directors Nominated Were:

Tarbert: *David Cameron, Steve McCombe, Barbara MacKay, and John Murdo Morrison (West Tarbert)*
Urgha to Glen Carragreich: *Duncan J MacLeod*
Kyles of Scalpay: *John Archie Macdonald*
Ardhasaig to Loch Meavaig: *Calum MacKay*
Meavaig to Huishinish: *Catherine Morrison*
Bowglass to Ardvourlie: *Murdo Morrison*

(Minute of NHT Meeting, Thursday 13th March.)

The newly-nominated directors were invited to a committee meeting on Wednesday 19th March, just before the Inaugural General Meeting. At the meeting, new office-bearers were elected. David Cameron, who had been Chairman throughout the interim period, proposed that Calum MacKay should be elected as Chair. The proposal was seconded by John Murdo Morrison (West Tarbert) and passed unanimously. While thanking everybody, Calum Mackay singled out two individuals in particular. First he thanked David Cameron for his real dedication, his commitment and the tremendous work which he had put into the negotiations. Second he thanked Duncan MacPherson for his ongoing work on behalf of the Trust. He also proposed that David Cameron be elected Vice-Chair, because he wanted to be able to call upon his experience. Steve McCombe seconded the proposal, which was passed unanimously. The John Muir Trust had already accepted an offer to become a member of the Trust, and had nominated Nigel Hawkins as Director with Will Boyd-Wallis as alternate. The Directors agreed to offer Ian Scarr-Hall personal nominated membership for as long as he was in possession of Amhuinnsuidhe Castle and the associated fishings, although this decision applied only to Ian Scarr-Hall in person, and did not set a precedent for any future owners of the Castle. The meeting requested that Duncan MacPherson should continue as Secretary until the Trust had its own personnel in place, and that he should also continue as Minute secretary until an administrator was appointed. The Old Hostel, Tarbert was to remain as the registered office. All those who had applied for membership, but had not been present at the Inaugural General Meeting, were admitted as members of the Trust. By 19th March, membership of the Trust stood at 219.

Other administrative details to be tied up at these meetings in early March included finalising the Trust website and arranging for as wide a distribution as possible of the Appeal leaflets. It was agreed to join the Tourist Board at a cost of £30-£50, as the Board would distribute Appeal leaflets to a wide cross-section of visitors.

While all these arrangements had to be made and necessary decisions had to be taken, probably the most exciting and rewarding topic was planning the programme for the Celebration Day. This had been fixed for Friday 21st March 2003, the day on which, at last, the land would belong to the community of North Harris. Over several meetings, the programme took shape. An afternoon programme based at the Scaladale Centre in the Ardvourlie area was chosen, for a number of good reasons. Most importantly, the Centre provided shelter if the weather was wet – a very necessary precaution at any time of year, but particularly in March! Scaladale also recommended itself because it had a long history related to the land struggle. The new Millennium Forest created there was an outstanding example of a crofter initiative, and Scaladale's proximity to the main road made for easy access and parking for everyone who wanted to attend the ceremony. Finally, Scaladale provided the benefit of a magnificent scenic backdrop of mountains on one side and the expanse of Loch Seaforth on the other.

In addition to the afternoon programme, an evening programme was planned, using two sites in Tarbert. A traditional ceilidh was to be held at one, and a more modern celebration for the younger population at the other. Thought was also given to arranging something suitable for the very young and the very old. Harris Hotel would do the catering and the Young Enterprise Group would be asked to take the sandwiches to the Scaladale Centre. A bus would be available to take older primary school pupils from Tarbert to Scaladale. The handover would be made to David Cameron, and Calum MacKay would be Master of Ceremonies. A Gaelic psalm would be sung as part of the thanksgiving service. Invitations were to be sent to all council members, to other communities where there had been buy-outs, such as Valtos, Assynt, Knoydart and a personal invitation to John MacKenzie of Assynt, who had been a friend since the very first public meeting of the community back in April 2002. Seonaidh Alec MacPherson would be *Fear an Taighe* (Master of Ceremonies) for the evening ceilidh.

Brian Wilson MP, Minister for Energy, had indicated that his Department might be able to provide some assistance to the Trust, and he expressed his wish to be there on the day. After consultation with other members of the group, David Cameron replied that funding for a comprehensive study of the potential for renewable energy generation on the estate would be welcome. (Minute of NHT Meeting, 19th March, 2002.)

On 17 March, just four days before the Celebration, David Cameron reported to a meeting of Directors that the deal was now complete and that the buy-out had been achieved on Friday 14th March 2003. He had attended what he described as a surprisingly low-key meeting in Edinburgh, where he had signed the necessary documents and seen the transfer of the money to pay for the deal. (Minute of NHT Meeting, 17th March 2003.)

It has been known for the weather in Harris to be as warm and balmy in March as on a summer day. Days when the mountains are etched like grey velvet against a Mediterranean blue sky do occur from time to time. Friday 21 March 2003 was not one of these. It was stormy as only the islands can be stormy. As has happened on many a momentous occasion in island history, a group of determined people stood on the moor defying the elements, this time to hear Simon Fraser enact the ancient ceremony of taking *sasine,* whereby the land is handed over from the old owner to a new owner. Handing over to David Cameron a symbolic sachet of stone and earth, Simon Fraser said, in words which invoked centuries of Scottish tradition,

> *'From time immemorial it was the custom and the law of Scotland that, when a new owner was given possession of land, this would be done in a ceremony held on the land itself. In this ceremony, in the presence of witnesses, stone and earth of that land would be handed to the new owner. The ceremony was known as giving sasine. An account of the ceremony was written down in Latin and that account recorded in the Register of Sasines. Through time, the recording of the written account became more important, and eventually the ceremony of sasine was abolished. It was, however, revived in Gigha last year and we are now going to bring it back to the Western Isles.*
>
> *I now call on David Cameron to receive sasine on behalf of the North Harris Trust.*
>
> *David Cameron, I hereby deliver into your hands stone and earth of this land, and in doing so give unto the North Harris Trust true and lawful sasine of these whole Lands of North Harris; from the low tide of the sea to the highest mountain tops, ab caelo usque ad centrum; to be held on behalf of the people of North Harris in all time coming; agus tha sinn uile a tha cruinn còmhla an seo an dràsda a' guidhe gu soirbhich leibh agus leis gach ginealach a tha ri teachd agus gum faigh sibh a h-uile beannachd anns an talamh seo a tha ar tighearna air a thoirt dhuibh ri shealbhachadh.*

*All we who are gathered together at this moment
pray that you and every generation to come will
prosper, and that you will receive every blessing on
this land which our Lord has given you to enjoy.'*

The Gaelic words eloquently articulated a sense of solidarity, of
gratitude that they had reached this moment, and the fervent
hope that the achievement would be blessed both for themselves
and for their children.

Twenty-two year old Joanna Morrison, whose family had
lived in close proximity to the Castle for generations, was chosen
to plant a commemorative tree. In her whole-hearted support
for the buy-out and the North Harris Trust, Joanna Morrison
reflected the change in attitudes of her generation, both to private
landownership and to the role of women beyond the domestic
arena. After the ceremony on the hillside it was a relief to enjoy
the warmth of the Scaladale Centre.

The historical atmosphere of the celebration, so effectively
established at the outdoor ceremony, was sustained inside the
Centre by the first speaker, Murdo Morrison of Ardvourlie. For
Murdo Morrison and those who shared his vision, at least some
of the significance of the day was rooted in memories handed
down by word of mouth over the generations. He reminded the
audience that they were standing just a couple of miles away
from the monument to those who had taken part in the Pàirc
Deer Raid a hundred and sixteen years earlier. During that
episode in the land struggle, a group of local cottars who lived in
congestion and near starvation, while all around them good land
was devoted to a deer forest, had petitioned the Estate for more
land. They were turned down repeatedly. In desperation, they
raided the deer forest on the other side of the loch. The army and
the navy were called in to deal with them, the Riot Act was read,
and sixteen men were arrested and charged with mobbing and
rioting. They were taken to Edinburgh to stand trial. Thanks to
a skilful defence, they were found not guilty. Murdo Morrison's
quietly-spoken account of that incident moved to tears those who
shared his conviction that possession of their own land was the
first essential for their future prosperity.

Among the official speeches, there were some important announcements. Allan Wilson, Deputy Environment and Rural Affairs Minister, referring to the gale outside (but with a serious message in the quip) told them that there was money to be reaped from the wind. Acknowledging that the Trust had to explore ways of 'turning a profit' on the land they had just acquired, he said that he now knew how wind power could refuel the regeneration of the Western Isles. (*WHFP* 28 March 2003.) Perhaps the most important news for the future of the North Harris Trust came from David Campbell, Chair of the Scottish Land Fund, who announced the award of £90,000 to enable the Trust to appoint both a Development Office and an Administrator.

Brian Wilson, UK Energy Minister, who had been a leader in the successful campaign for land reform in Scotland, expressed his pleasure at the success of the buy-out.

> '*Until recently, it was a prospect which did not even feature in our dreams and aspirations. North Harris was a bastion that would never crumble; a symbol of Hebridean landlordism... If anyone doubts that the trickle of land reform in the Highlands is going to become a tide, then they should observe what has happened in North Harris over the past few months. Ownership and management of these estates, by the people who live on them, is a noble concept whose time has come.*'
> (*WHFP* 28 March 2003.)

There were congratulatory messages from Highlands and Islands Enterprise Community Land Unit, from the New Opportunities Scottish Land Fund and from the John Muir Trust, who had all contributed so much to the success of the buy-out. Ian Scarr-Hall, whose partnership made it possible for the North Harris Trust to buy the land without the Castle, was there – but typically sought no credit for himself. Willie McSporran, Chairman of the Isle of Gigha Trust, sent a message of encouragement to the North Harris Trust, saying:

'Since any of us can remember, the destinies of our communities have lain in the hands of others. This is no more. We now have the authority to plan our own path, to make our own way. On Saturday (the first anniversary of the Gigha buy-out) we likened our island's development under community ownership to the growth of a tree. Already we can see the flowering buds, but it will be in the future years that we will see the full fruits of our labours.'

The afternoon ceremony ended with a short service of thanksgiving and the singing of Psalm 24 in Gaelic, verses which echoed once more the sentiment expressed in the opening prayer at the first public meeting in April 2002:

'S le Dia an talamh is a làn an dòmhain 's na bheil ann - The earth belongs unto the Lord, and all that it contains.'

Profound gratitude, a sober sense of responsibility and faith in the future were the dominant features of the celebration as the lands of North Harris passed into community ownership.

Postscript

When, in December 1994, North Harris Estate Limited (i.e. the Bulmer family) bought North Harris from Mrs Panchaud – or rather from Enessy Co. S.A., to use the wording in the Disposition – an area of land with the mineral rights, comprising some 7,472 acres in the north-east of the estate, was retained by the sellers. The area which came to be called the Seaforth Estate bordered on the shores of Loch Seaforth and included the small villages of Rhenigidale, Eileananabuich, Scaladale and a portion of land at Maaruig. As it happens, Loch Seaforth has the largest deep water anchorage on the east coast of Lewis and Harris. The exclusion of this area around Loch Seaforth from the sale of the rest of North Harris was made in the context of a current planning application by Redland Aggregates Ltd. for a coastal superquarry at Rodel. At the time there was a strong demand for aggregates, and plans for a number of coastal superquarries were postulated: for example, there were plans from another company seeking to quarry a huge chamber into the hill near Miavaig.

Whatever plans for developing a superquarry on the shores of Loch Seaforth there may have been in 1994, these fell by the wayside when, after a long Inquiry, the application for a superquarry at Lingerbay near Rodel was eventually turned down. The tiny Seaforth Estate, consisting of only twenty-one crofts, became something of an anomaly. The residents of the Seaforth Estate were keen that it should be re-united with North Harris. The Seaforth Estate Steering Group was chaired by Kenny MacKay, the same gentleman who had been the first Chairman of the North Harris Community Steering Group – which must be a record in the history of community buy-outs. In March 2006, after fifteen months negotiation, and with the help of Simon Fraser and the Community Land Unit (CLU) in the persons of Sandra Holmes and Donnie MacKay, the North Harris Trust acquired the Seaforth Estate. This acquisition fulfilled a long-held wish that the land mass of North Harris should be re-united as one estate under community ownership, a fitting postscript to the brave decision taken in Tarbert in 2002.

Bibliography

Primary Sources:

Chambers Biographical Dictionary, Revised Edition, (Chambers, Edinburgh, 1969)
Community Land Unit files and correspondence with (a) North Harris
Community Steering Group and (b) North Harris Trust.
Dé Tha Dol? Newsletter of Harris Voluntary Service.
Highlands and Islands Enterprise Home Page and relevant links.
Highlands and Islands Enterprise, Community Land Ownership.
Highlands and Islands Enterprise, *The Community Right to Buy-your questions answered: Part 2 of the Land Reform (Scotland) Act 2003.*
Highlands and Islands Enterprise: Community Land Unit, *Tir na Gaidhealtachd: Action Framework, 2001-2002*, Revised June 2002.
John Muir Trust, *Journal and News, No. 34, Partnership in North Harris*, Winter, 2003.
New Opportunities Fund, *Scottish Land Fund: Ionmhas Fearainn Na h-Alba, Guidance Notes: Green Spaces and Sustainable Communities.*
North Harris Trust Feasibility Study.
North Harris Trust, Memorandum and Articles of Association.
North Harris Community Steering Group, Minutes of Meetings and correspondence.
North Harris Trust, Minutes of Meetings, legal papers and diverse correspondence re purchase of the North Harris Estate.
Royal Commission on the Highlands and Islands, 1883 (Report of the Napier Commission).
Scottish Land Fund Files and correspondence with North Harris Community Steering Group and North Harris Trust, SCL/140
 Scottish Natural Heritage Files and correspondence with North Harris Trust.

Third Statistical Account of Scotland: County of Inverness: Outer Isles District: Parish of Harris, Vol. XVI, H. Barron, ed., (Scottish Academic Press, 1985)

Secondary Sources:

Devine, T. M., *Great Highland Famine: Hunger, Emigration and the Scottish Highlands in the Nineteenth Century* (John Donald, Edinburgh, 2003)
Duncan, Angus, *Hebridean Island: Memories of Scarp,* A. Duncan Ed. (Tuckwell Press, East Linton, 1995)
Hunter, James, *The Making of the Crofting Community* (John Donald, Edinburgh, 1976)
Hutchinson, Roger, *The Soap Man: Lewis, Harris and Lord Leverhulme* (Birlinn Ltd., 2003)
Lawson, Bill, *Harris Families and How to Trace Them,* (Northton, 1990)
Lawson, Bill, *Harris in History and Legend* (John Donald, Edinburgh, 2002)
Leneman, Leah, *Fit for Heroes* (Aberdeen, 1989)
MacAskill, John, *We have Won the Land; the story of the purchase by the Assynt Crofters' Trust of the North Lochinver Estate* (Acair, Stornoway, 1999)
Mackenzie, W.C. *History of the Outer Hebrides,* (Alexander Gardener, Paisley, 1903)
Macphail, I.M.M. *The Crofters' War* (Acair, Stornoway, 1989)
Nicolson, Nigel *Lord of the Isles: Lord: Leverhulme in the Hebrides* (London, 1960)
Scherr, Tony, leaflet on history of Harris, 2003.
Wightman, A.D. *Who Owns Scotland?* (Canongate Books, Edinburgh, 1996)

Newspapers:

Aberdeen Press and Journal
Daily Telegraph
Herald
Observer

Scotland on Sunday
Scotsman
Stornoway Gazette
West Highland Free Press

Index